An Analysis of

Eric Foner's

Reconstruction
America's Unfinished Revolution, 1863–1877

T0301896

Jason Xidias

Published by Macat International Ltd
24:13 Coda Centre, 189 Munster Road, London SW6 6AW.

Distributed exclusively by Routledge
2 Park Square, Milton Park, Abingdon, Oxon OX14 4RN
711 Third Avenue, New York, NY 10017, USA

Routledge is an imprint of the Taylor & Francis Group, an informa business

www.macat.com
info@macat.com

Cataloguing in Publication Data
A catalogue record for this book is available from the British Library.
Library of Congress Cataloguing-in-Publication Data is available upon request.
Cover illustration: Kim Thompson

ISBN 978-1-912302-55-0 (hardback)
ISBN 978-1-912128-22-8 (paperback)
ISBN 978-1-912281-43-5 (e-book)

Notice
The information in this book is designed to orientate readers of the work under analysis,
to elucidate and contextualise its key ideas and themes, and to aid in the development
of critical thinking skills. It is not meant to be used, nor should it be used, as a
substitute for original thinking or in place of original writing or research. References and
notes are provided for informational purposes and their presence does not constitute
endorsement of the information or opinions therein. This book is presented solely for
educational purposes. It is sold on the understanding that the publisher is not engaged
to provide any scholarly advice. The publisher has made every effort to ensure that
this book is accurate and up-to-date, but makes no warranties or representations with
regard to the completeness or reliability of the information it contains. The information
and the opinions provided herein are not guaranteed or warranted to produce particular
results and may not be suitable for students of every ability. The publisher shall not be
liable for any loss, damage or disruption arising from any errors or omissions, or from
the use of this book, including, but not limited to, special, incidental, consequential or
other damages caused, or alleged to have been caused, directly or indirectly, by the
information contained within.

CONTENTS

WAYS IN TO THE TEXT

Who Was Eric Foner?   9

What Does *Reconstruction* Say?   10

Why Does *Reconstruction* Matter?   12

SECTION 1: INFLUENCES

Module 1: The Author and the Historical Context   16

Module 2: Academic Context   21

Module 3: The Problem   26

Module 4: The Author's Contribution   30

SECTION 2: IDEAS

Module 5: Main Ideas   36

Module 6: Secondary Ideas   42

Module 7: Achievement   47

Module 8: Place in the Author's Work   51

SECTION 3: IMPACT

Module 9: The First Responses   56

Module 10: The Evolving Debate   60

Module 11: Impact and Influence Today   64

Module 12: Where Next?   68

Glossary of Terms   73

People Mentioned in the Text   84

Works Cited   90

THE MACAT LIBRARY

The Macat Library is a series of unique academic explorations of seminal works in the humanities and social sciences – books and papers that have had a significant and widely recognised impact on their disciplines. It has been created to serve as much more than just a summary of what lies between the covers of a great book. It illuminates and explores the influences on, ideas of, and impact of that book. Our goal is to offer a learning resource that encourages critical thinking and fosters a better, deeper understanding of important ideas.

Each publication is divided into three Sections: Influences, Ideas, and Impact. Each Section has four Modules. These explore every important facet of the work, and the responses to it.

This Section-Module structure makes a Macat Library book easy to use, but it has another important feature. Because each Macat book is written to the same format, it is possible (and encouraged!) to cross-reference multiple Macat books along the same lines of inquiry or research. This allows the reader to open up interesting interdisciplinary pathways.

To further aid your reading, lists of glossary terms and people mentioned are included at the end of this book (these are indicated by an asterisk [*] throughout) – as well as a list of works cited.

Macat has worked with the University of Cambridge to identify the elements of critical thinking and understand the ways in which six different skills combine to enable effective thinking.
Three allow us to fully understand a problem; three more give us the tools to solve it. Together, these six skills make up the **PACIER** model of critical thinking. They are:

ANALYSIS – understanding how an argument is built
EVALUATION – exploring the strengths and weaknesses of an argument
INTERPRETATION – understanding issues of meaning

CREATIVE THINKING – coming up with new ideas and fresh connections
PROBLEM-SOLVING – producing strong solutions
REASONING – creating strong arguments

To find out more, visit **WWW.MACAT.COM.**

CRITICAL THINKING AND *RECONSTRUCTION IN AMERICA*

Primary critical thinking skill: PROBLEM-SOLVING
Secondary critical thinking skill: REASONING

'Reconstruction' is the name given to the period that, beginning shortly before the end of the American Civil War and running until 1877, saw the frustration of federal government's attempts to integrate the newly freed slaves into the American political and economic system. It ended in frustration, disillusionment and also violence, with individual southern states denying rights to freed slaves, preventing them from voting, and largely forcing them back into roles that exploited their labor and prevented them from gaining access to education. For much of the 20th century, the predominant view of the Reconstruction period was that of the Dunning School, which argued that former slaves were unprepared for the responsibilities of voting and holding office, and that it was their incapability of handling such responsibilities – and not the racist actions of whites – that was largely responsible for the failures of the Reconstruction period. Eric Foner's great work reverses those judgements.

Foner adopts a problem-solving approach, asking productive questions of state archives and generating and assessing alternative possibilities to assess the views of the Dunning School in a much wider context. His verdict – that slaves and freedmen were often key figures who shaped the eventual emergence of a more progressive American democracy – is backed up by persuasive reasoning which explains how these results came about and shows how the white establishment, led by President Andrew Johnson, was primarily responsible for the disasters of the Reconstruction era.

ABOUT THE AUTHOR OF THE ORIGINAL WORK

Eric Foner is one of the foremost scholars of the American Civil War (1861–65) and is widely recognized as the leading contemporary historian of Reconstruction, the period following the Civil War between 1865 and 1877 when the US struggled to reunify and integrate millions of newly freed slaves. Born in New York City in 1943 into a family of prominent historians, Foner's writing has deepened popular and academic understanding of this pivotal period in American history. He has written or edited over 20 books and has received many prestigious awards for his work, including the Lincoln Prize, the Bancroft Prize, and the coveted Pulitzer Prize.

ABOUT THE AUTHORS OF THE ANALYSIS

Dr Jason Xidias holds a PhD in European Politics from King's College London, where he completed a comparative dissertation on immigration and citizenship in Britain and France. He was also a Visiting Fellow in European Politics at the University of California, Berkeley. Currently, he is Lecturer in Political Science at New York University.

ABOUT MACAT

GREAT WORKS FOR CRITICAL THINKING

Macat is focused on making the ideas of the world's great thinkers accessible and comprehensible to everybody, everywhere, in ways that promote the development of enhanced critical thinking skills.

It works with leading academics from the world's top universities to produce new analyses that focus on the ideas and the impact of the most influential works ever written across a wide variety of academic disciplines. Each of the works that sit at the heart of its growing library is an enduring example of great thinking. But by setting them in context – and looking at the influences that shaped their authors, as well as the responses they provoked – Macat encourages readers to look at these classics and game-changers with fresh eyes. Readers learn to think, engage and challenge their ideas, rather than simply accepting them.

'Macat offers an amazing first-of-its-kind tool for interdisciplinary learning and research. Its focus on works that transformed their disciplines and its rigorous approach, drawing on the world's leading experts and educational institutions, opens up a world-class education to anyone.'

Andreas Schleicher
Director for Education and Skills, Organisation for Economic
Co-operation and Development

'Macat is taking on some of the major challenges in university education … They have drawn together a strong team of active academics who are producing teaching materials that are novel in the breadth of their approach.'

Prof Lord Broers,
former Vice-Chancellor of the University of Cambridge

'The Macat vision is exceptionally exciting. It focuses upon new modes of learning which analyse and explain seminal texts which have profoundly influenced world thinking and so social and economic development. It promotes the kind of critical thinking which is essential for any society and economy.
This is the learning of the future.'

Rt Hon Charles Clarke, former UK Secretary of State for Education

'The Macat analyses provide immediate access to the critical conversation surrounding the books that have shaped their respective discipline, which will make them an invaluable resource to all of those, students and teachers, working in the field.'

Professor William Tronzo, University of California at San Diego

WAYS IN TO THE TEXT

KEY POINTS

- Born in 1943, Eric Foner is regarded as an important scholar of the American Civil War* and Reconstruction.* (The American Civil War was fought in the United States between the Northern* and Southern* states from 1861 to 1865. "Reconstruction" is the name given to the period from 1865 to 1877 when the federal government of the United States reincorporated the Southern states into the Union.)

- *In Reconstruction: America's Unfinished Revolution, 1863–1877,* Foner went against previously held views by arguing that African Americans, rather than whites, were the primary force in shaping the abolition* of slavery in the period after the Civil War.

- Foner uses evidence from previously untapped state archives to deliver the most meticulous and coherent study produced to date on the era of Reconstruction.

Who Is Eric Foner?

Eric Foner, the author of *Reconstruction: America's Unfinished Revolution, 1863–1877* (1988) was born in New York City in 1943. Today, he is widely recognized as one of the leading scholars of the American Civil War and as the leading contemporary historian of the era known as Reconstruction that followed it. During Reconstruction, the government of the victorious Union* (Northern) states directed the

Confederate* (Southern) states to rebuild their social institutions with a view to those states' reincorporation into the federal system; the rights of former slaves were significant in this process.

Foner comes from a family of prominent historians. His father, Jack Foner,* was a professor of history at City College of New York, and specialized in labor movements and civil rights.* His uncle, Philip Foner,* was also a professor of history at City College of New York, and the author and editor of more than 100 books, including an influential five-volume set on the life and legacy of Frederick Douglass,* a slave who escaped captivity and became the most important black leader of the nineteenth century.

Eric Foner has enjoyed a distinguished academic career, principally spent at City University of New York (CUNY) and, since 1982, at Columbia University. He is the author or editor of more than 20 books and the recipient of several prestigious awards for his writing, including the Pulitzer Prize for History in 2011. He is also a former president of the Organization of American Historians and the American Historical Association.

What Does *Reconstruction: America's Unfinished Revolution, 1863–1877* Say?

Eric Foner identifies the starting point of Reconstruction as 1863 and its end as 1877. He describes this 14-year period as an idealistic, ultimately failed, democratic* experiment intended to quickly integrate emancipated* (liberated) slaves as equal citizens. Furthermore, as the title of the book suggests, Foner believes that the African American struggle for freedom and equality is an "unfinished revolution." Black people in the United States had to wait almost another century before achieving full legal equality; they continue to face racial discrimination and inequalities even today.

In *Reconstruction*, Foner cleverly weaves archival research with secondary sources to present a convincing story. By putting slaves and emancipated slaves at the heart of his analysis, he moves away from previous scholarship, arguing that it was these African Americans who were the main drivers of the abolition of slavery in the US in 1865, and the obtaining of legal rights. In particular, Foner emphasizes the key role freed slaves played in the Northern military during the Civil War (1861–65), while also highlighting how their struggles for legal rights during the Reconstruction period (1865–77) created new understandings of democracy, labor, and even identity.

The legal rights won by African Americans when slavery ended lasted only a short time under the frequently violent pressure of white Southern defiance; for example, from 1865 they gradually lost the right to vote. Foner shows how Reconstruction radically transformed our understanding of masters and slaves, highlighting many of the era's forgotten achievements (he reminds us, for example, that a small number of African Americans serving in the Northern military were elected to political office for the first time).

Reconstruction, the conclusion of a half century of scholarship on the subject, has disproved the idea that white people were entirely responsible for the advances African Americans made from 1863 to 1877. According to this interpretation, black people were not themselves able to effect change, and failed to acknowledge how their own struggles actively shaped progress in the United States. Foner's research has further discredited the once-dominant theory that black people were naturally inferior to white people and that was why they were incapable of freeing themselves. William A. Dunning,* a well-known historian and political scientist at Columbia University, made this claim to give intellectual validity to Jim Crow*—a set of laws passed in the post-Reconstruction period, mostly by Southern states, that established and reinforced racial segregation in public places. These laws were effective from 1890 until the 1960s, and were a major force undermining the potential gains of Reconstruction.

Foner's conclusion is that, overall, Reconstruction was a failure because the white establishment prevented African Americans from becoming equal citizens. In particular, he criticizes then-president Andrew Johnson* for failing to redistribute lands taken during the Civil War to freedmen (former slaves), rather than returning them to their original white owners, who then established a sharecropping* system in the postwar South. Sharecropping was a labor system that replaced slavery after 1863. Initially, plantation owners rented a portion of their land to former slaves, allowing them to use that land as they saw fit and to benefit from their own harvest. After 1865, Johnson made law reforms whereby black people became "employees" of plantation owners, in effect losing their independence and the right to benefit from their own harvest. Most former slaves had no land of their own, no money, and were barred from working elsewhere by the Black Codes,* laws passed by Southern states in 1865 and 1866 that restored white supremacy in the South after emancipation. They had no choice but to return to the plantations, where their former white masters continued to persecute them.

While Foner believes Reconstruction was a failure generally, he points out some positives. In particular, he highlights the fact that some black people were able to access public education for the first time, and others who served in the Northern military went on to hold political office. He also says that the struggles of freed slaves and of the white Radical Republicans*—a faction of the Republican Party from around 1854 to 1877 who advocated an end to slavery and equal rights for African Americans—established the context for the gains African Americans have since made in the twentieth and twenty-first centuries.

Finally, Foner draws on examples from state archives to show that, contrary to arguments of previous scholarship, in fact there was a significant level of interracial cooperation during this period. For example, he describes the progressive efforts of carpetbaggers* (Northerners who moved to the South after the war) and scalawags*

(Southern whites who supported the Union and abolition of slavery) who struggled to build a more equal society.

Why Does *Reconstruction: America's Unfinished Revolution, 1863–1877* Matter?

Foner describes Reconstruction as a period in which there was great tension between a well-established economic and social system in the South built on the oppression of black people, and a desire among African Americans and forward-thinking whites to build a more equal society. On the one hand, the struggles of freed slaves and white Radical Republicans led to the passing of the Civil Rights Acts of 1866* and 1875* and to the Thirteenth* (1865), Fourteenth* (1868), and Fifteenth* Amendments (1870) to the nation's Constitution* (the legal document setting out the nation's laws, the obligations of the government, and the rights of the people). Together, these laws granted African Americans equal civil and political rights.

On the other hand, beginning in 1865 Southern states used a variety of laws and scare tactics to prevent black people (and some poor whites) from actually making use of these rights. After the Southern Democrats* (the conservative Democratic Party in the Southern states who defended slavery) managed to win the congressional elections of 1874 and the majority in the House of Representatives* (one of the two legislative chambers of the United States Congress), they were able to gradually put an end to Radical Reconstruction,* the groundbreaking reforms in favor of African Americans that took place from 1863 to 1877. Where the federal (national) government awarded rights, the individual states denied black people those rights.

Reconstruction capitalizes on extensive and newly discovered state archives to present the most thorough and coherent analysis to date of this period. Alongside other revisionist* scholarship, which reinterprets older established ideas or assumptions, Foner discredits the traditional view that freed slaves played no role in the successes of Reconstruction and were responsible for its failures. This perspective, crafted by the Dunning School,* served as an ideological justification for racism and segregation.* William A. Dunning and others argued that granting black people the right to vote and hold office was a serious error, because they were both unprepared for and incapable of handling such responsibility.

Foner's book is important for the ways in which he portrays slaves and freedmen as key figures who shaped a more progressive American democracy. He highlights two main ways in which this came about. First, as Northern troops advanced in the South, plantation owners were forced to abandon their lands, and slaves rushed to Union lines, where they enlisted in the Northern military. So the war was not only a struggle to preserve the United States, but was also a fight to abolish slavery. Second, during Reconstruction, freed slaves developed a political consciousness based on a common history of racial discrimination, and collectively built up institutions and associations as a way of confronting discrimination and violence in an organized manner.

Reconstruction is widely recognized as a major work on the American Civil War and Reconstruction, and is an essential text for anyone who wants to know more about these key periods in American history. It is particularly relevant today as African Americans are even now still struggling to gain greater freedom and equality.

SECTION 1
INFLUENCES

MODULE 1
THE AUTHOR AND THE HISTORICAL CONTEXT

KEY POINTS

- Eric Foner is widely recognized as one of the leading scholars of the American Civil War* and as the leading historian of the Reconstruction* period that followed it.

- *Reconstruction* discredited influential interpretations of the period by arguing that slaves and freed slaves were the primary force behind the abolition* of slavery and the successes of Reconstruction from 1863 to 1877.

- The text remains significant today because Reconstruction is a key period in American history and because African Americans continue to struggle for greater freedom and equality.

Why Read This Text?

In *Reconstruction: America's Unfinished Revolution, 1863–1877* (1988), Eric Foner details why the Civil War and Reconstruction are important and highly controversial periods in American history. The former resulted in the abolition of slavery and the preservation of the United States, and the latter resulted in the reintegration of the 11 Southern states that had seceded* (withdrawn) from the Union* and the restructuring of their political, legal, and economic systems. Furthermore, Foner explains that Reconstruction was a radical experiment in interracial democracy quickly built from slavery, and was a period during which African Americans went on to obtain equal legal rights.

In *Reconstruction*, Foner emphasizes the central role African

❝ I just learned from my father a different way of thinking about American history, where race was the fundamental problem of America, where radical movements were tremendously important in changing American society ... My uncle Philip Foner was a very prolific historian. He created Frederick Douglass.* In 1950 or so he put together four volumes—no one had ever heard of Frederick Douglass at that time ... Today, every textbook talks about Frederick Douglass. ❞

Eric Foner, "Interview with Martha Abreu* and Hebe Mattos*"

Americans played in shaping these radical changes in American democracy. He also details the ways in which Northern industrialists and investors attempted to extend their free labor ideology* in the South. The Northern economic model rested on the idea that all individuals should have the right to a basic education and the ideals of equal opportunity and social mobility. In other words, they promised that, with hard work, "the wage laborer could rise to the status of independent farmer and craftsman."[1]

Foner describes how, determined to restore slavery, Southern plantation owners and the Ku Klux Klan* (a white supremacist organization established in 1866) defied this ideology and the progressive legislation passed by the Radical Republicans.*

He goes on to explain how the great depression of 1873*—the worst economic depression in American history up to that point— together with the 1874 congressional victory of the Southern Democrats* (a political faction opposed to the granting of rights to black Americans) prompted a change in the North's attitude and behavior. By 1877, President Rutherford B. Hayes* and others gave up on Reconstruction and removed Northern troops from the South. This allowed former Confederate* officials and slave-owners to return to power. When they did, they established the Black Codes,* voter restrictions, and imposed a sharecropping* system that reestablished an oppressive relationship between white plantation owners and black laborers. This, together with a conservative Supreme Court* that decided on a series of cases granting the Southern states more power to exploit African Americans, removed most of the gains that the emancipated* slaves and Radical Republicans had won.

Author's Life

Eric Foner was born in New York City on February 7, 1943. Career-wise he followed the example of his father, Jack Foner,* a history professor who specialized in civil rights* and the American labor movement, and his uncle, Philip Foner,* who was also a history professor, civil rights activist, and the author and editor of more than 100 books. Eric Foner is now regarded as one of the foremost contemporary scholars of the American Civil War and Reconstruction.

Foner completed a BA in history at Columbia University in 1963, another BA at Oxford University in 1965, and a PhD at Columbia University in 1969. From 1973 to 1982, he was professor of history at City University of New York, and since 1982 he has been DeWitt Clinton Professor of History at Columbia University. He has also worked as a visiting professor at the University of South Carolina, Cambridge University, Oxford University, Queen Mary University of London, and Moscow State University.

He is the author or editor of over 20 books, the most acclaimed of which have been *Free Soil, Free Labor, and Free Men* (1970); *Reconstruction: America's Unfinished Revolution 1863–1877* (1988), which won the Bancroft Prize* for works of history; and *The Fiery Trial: Abraham Lincoln and American Slavery* (2011), which was awarded the Pulitzer Prize* for History, the Lincoln Prize,* and the Bancroft Prize. In addition, Foner is the former president of the Organization of American Historians (1993–4) and the American Historical Association (2000).

Author's Background

Richard Morris,* a distinguished historian at Columbia University, invited Eric Foner to write *Reconstruction* for the prestigious *New American Nation Series* in 1975. Morris's invitation came as something of a surprise to Foner because he had not worked specifically on Reconstruction previously. His prior research had dealt with the causes of the Civil War, African American history (broadly speaking), the Anglo-American political writer Thomas Paine* (1737–1809), and radicalism.*

Foner identifies 1978 as a turning point in his research on Reconstruction. During his semester as a visiting scholar at the University of South Carolina, he discovered 121 boxes of untapped correspondence from the period 1863 to 1877. In these documents, he writes, "I read of utopian hopes and shattered dreams, struggles for human dignity and terrorist violence, racism and black–white cooperation, and how everyday life had become politicized in ways barely hinted at in the Reconstruction literature."[2]

Another key moment in the project came in 1980–1 when Foner was working as a visiting professor of American history at Cambridge University. Some of his British colleagues urged him to read literature about the abolition* of slavery in the British Empire.* In the process, he discovered fresh angles to explore in aspects of slave emancipation that American historians had overlooked. In particular, Foner recalls becoming aware of the interplay between economics and racism. That is, he gained a much deeper insight into the tension between the pursuit of liberated slaves for economic freedom and social mobility, and the defiance of white property-owners to safeguard their power and privileges.

After discovering and amassing such a wealth and breadth of primary sources during the course of this research project, Foner decided to continue deepening his understanding of the American

NOTES

1   Eric Foner, *Reconstruction: America's Unfinished Revolution, 1863–1877* (New York: HarperCollins, 2014), 29.

2   Foner, *Reconstruction*, xxix.

MODULE 2
ACADEMIC CONTEXT

KEY POINTS

- In *Reconstruction*, Eric Foner uses rare, firsthand accounts of the era to show that African American slaves and freedmen (newly freed slaves) were central to the abolition* of slavery and the successes of the Reconstruction* era that followed the American Civil War.*

- With its challenge to dominant historical assumptions, the social theorist W. E. B. Du Bois's* *Black Reconstruction in America* (1935) was the first major revisionist* text on Reconstruction and a major influence on Foner.

- *Reconstruction* presents evidence that discredits influential interpretations of the period—notably that of the Dunning School*—to present the most complete and convincing analysis of this vital historical period in American history.

The Work in Its Context

Eric Foner's *Reconstruction: America's Unfinished Revolution, 1863–1877* challenges the Dunning School, the dominant historical interpretation of Reconstruction until after World War II.*

During Reconstruction, the North reintegrated the 11 Southern states* that had seceded* from the United States and restructured their political, legal, and economic systems. Its reforms included legal protections and new civil rights* for freed slaves that Congress* (the lawmaking body of the US government) incorporated into the Thirteenth,* Fourteenth,* and Fifteenth Amendments* to the Constitution* of the United States.

The Columbia University professor William A. Dunning* and his

> **&& The slave went free; stood a brief moment in the sun; then moved back again toward slavery. ??**
>
> W. E. B. Du Bois, *Black Reconstruction in America*

followers had argued that black people were too immature to be freed from slavery, and were not intelligent enough to exercise the equal legal rights granted to them in Reconstruction, particularly the right to vote and hold political office. Furthermore, he asserted that Reconstruction had ruined the South and that segregation was the best means of safeguarding "white civilized society."

During the course of the twentieth century, revisionist critics challenged this perspective, attacking Dunning's flimsy arguments, and gradually revealing the realities of Reconstruction. The earliest of these revisionists (critics who challenge orthodox historical interpretation) was W. E. B. Du Bois, the first African American to graduate from Harvard University and the editor of *Crisis* magazine,* published by the civil rights organization National Association for the Advancement of Colored People (NAACP).* In 1935 Du Bois published *Black Reconstruction in America*, in which he argued that white people, rather than African Americans, had been responsible for the failures of Reconstruction. He detailed the defiance of Southern plantation owners and the profound violence of the white supremacist organization the Ku Klux Klan,* and showed how these two elements, rather than alleged black incompetence, led to Jim Crow*—the system of racial segregation that remained in place until the mid-1960s. Du Bois made it clear that the Southern agricultural economy was built on the exploitation of black people, and that material greed was the primary cause of racism and disenfranchisement* (the state of not being able to vote).

Foner has advanced Du Bois's work and the scholarship of other revisionists—like Kenneth Stampp*—by further detailing the interplay between economics and racism, and attributing the failures of Reconstruction to Southern defiance and violence, and a lack of strong Northern opposition after 1877. In this regard, *Reconstruction* has further discredited the faulty and thoroughly racist interpretation of the Dunning School.

Overview of the Field

The Dunning School, a key part of the intellectual establishment that justified and sustained racism and segregation, was the dominant interpretation of the Reconstruction era until the end of World War II.* Dunning and his disciplines argued that granting black people the right to vote and hold political office was a serious error because they were unprepared for, and fundamentally incapable of, handling such responsibilities. This perspective is an example of how social scientists adapted the nineteenth-century naturalist Charles Darwin's* ideas on evolutionary biology* to argue that white people were innately superior to black people.

Foner is forceful in his description of the destructive impact of the Dunning School: "All of the alleged horrors of Reconstruction helped to freeze the minds of the white South in resistance to any change whatsoever … For a long time it was an intellectual straitjacket for much of the white South, and historians have a lot to answer for in helping to propagate a racist system in this country."[1]

Du Bois's *Black Reconstruction in America* was the first prominent sociological text to discredit Dunning's interpretation. It describes racism as a social construction designed to advance the material interests of white property-owners by encouraging poor whites and black people to see each other as competition rather than having shared interests to fight together. Although his book received little attention when it was first published, revisionist scholars revived Du Bois's work in the second half of the twentieth century in light of the Holocaust* (the mass murder of minorities, chiefly Jewish people, in

Europe during World War II), anticolonial struggles in Africa, and the Civil Rights movement* in the United States.

In *Reconstruction*, Foner reinforces Du Bois's conclusions by drawing on new primary research, asking innovative questions, and providing a detailed, objective account of the period without the established assumptions based on Dunning's racist logic. In an effort to finally bury the Dunning School, Foner details how African Americans were the driving force behind abolition and the successes of Reconstruction.

Academic Influences

Although Foner originally majored in physics at Columbia University, he changed to history after taking a year-long course with the historian James Shenton* on the American Civil War and Reconstruction. As Foner recalls, Shenton was an animated lecturer (in addition to being a professor, he also narrated historical documentaries on American television) who motivated him to learn even more about these periods in American history. The course, he says, "probably determined that most of my career has been focused on that period."[2]

Another important academic influence was Foner's PhD supervisor, Richard Hofstadter,* who he describes as "the premier historian of his generation."[3] Hofstadter preceded Foner as Dewitt Clinton Professor of American History at Columbia University, and has written several important works, including *The Age of Reform* (1955), which won the Pulitzer Prize the following year.

Foner's doctoral dissertation, *Free Soil, Free Labor, Free Men: The Ideology of the Republican Party before the Civil War*, analyzed the key factors that shaped the Northern majority's opposition to slavery and its ultimate decision to go to war. His original perspective on the subject resulted in his first two journal publications in 1965 and a book in 1970. These publications positioned him as a recognized scholar of the American Civil War.

NOTES

1   Mike Konczal, "How Radical Change Occurs: An Interview with Historian Eric
    Foner," *The Nation*, February 3, 2015, accessed December 9, 2015, http://
    www.thenation.com/article/how-radical-change-occurs-interview-historian-
    eric-foner/

2   Eric Watkin, "Professor James P. Shenton '49: History's Happy Warrior,"
    Columbia College Today 22, no. 3 (1996).

3   Eric Foner, *Who Owns History? Rethinking the Past in a Changing World*
    (New York: Hill and Wang, 2002), part I.

MODULE 3
THE PROBLEM

KEY POINTS

- *In Reconstruction*, Eric Foner's aim is to better understand what shaped abolition* and the successes and failures of the period following the American Civil War.*

- Foner builds on the work of the social theorist W. E. B. Du Bois,* the historian Kenneth Stampp,* and other revisionists* to provide a convincing analysis of Reconstruction* that disproves the assumptions of racist accounts of this period in history.

- Foner argues that African Americans, rather than white people, were central to the abolition of slavery and the successes of Reconstruction, and that white people, rather than African Americans, were responsible for its failures.

Core Question

Eric Foner's *Reconstruction: America's Unfinished Revolution, 1863–1877* addresses several important questions regarding the Civil War and Reconstruction. In particular, Foner wanted to explore who and what really prompted the end of slavery, and where the credit for Reconstruction's successes and failures should be placed.

Foner explains that these questions are highly complex and historiographically* controversial (historiography is the study of how history is researched and written, including the cultural assumptions, prejudices, and agendas of historians). His objective, like the revisionist scholars who came before him, is to bury once and for all the inaccurate and racist interpretations put forward by the historian William A. Dunning.* Foner's research shows that African Americans, rather than white elites, were the ones primarily responsible for the

❝ Blacks appeared either as passive victims of white manipulation or as an unthinking people whose 'animal natures' threatened the stability of civilized society. ❞

Eric Foner, *Reconstruction: America's Unfinished Revolution, 1863–1877*

movements that led to President Abraham Lincoln's Emancipation* Proclamation* in 1863 (outlawing slavery in the United States), and for the positive developments of Reconstruction. In addition, he asserts that Reconstruction failed because of the defiance of Southern plantation owners, the violence of the Ku Klux Klan* and other white supremacist* groups, and the decision by the North to remove its troops from the South in 1877.

Prior to the work of revisionists, scholars of the then-dominant Dunning School* had ignored the evidence that existed on black activism during this period. Instead, they offered a pseudoscientific, racist explanation for the failure of Reconstruction that black people were innately incapable of coping with their newfound freedom. Foner's meticulous and logical analysis has advanced the work of revisionists such as W. E. B. Du Bois, Kenneth Stampp,* and Howard Beale,* and has redefined how historians understand and teach the American Civil War and Reconstruction.

The Participants

Research on Reconstruction began with the work of William A. Dunning and the political scientist John Burgess,* and continued with the students they taught at Columbia University. These two scholars developed what later became known as the Dunning School, which suggested that whites—rather than blacks—were responsible for realizing abolition and the successes of Reconstruction. This interpretation was dominant from the beginning of the twentieth century until the end of World War II.*

Du Bois's *Black Reconstruction in America* (1935) challenged the Dunning School by arguing that whites, rather than African Americans, were responsible for the failures of Reconstruction. Du Bois was the first prominent scholar to place the emancipated slave at the heart of his research. He described Reconstruction as a period of intense struggle over economic resources. In particular, black people were fighting for freedom and social mobility, and white plantation-owners were attempting to restore slavery (or similar systems of racialized labor exploitation) in order to safeguard their power and privileges.

Du Bois's work, along with other important revisionist contributions that followed it, such as Stampp's *The Peculiar Institution* (1956) and *The Era of Reconstruction, 1865–1877* (1965), took the Dunning School and its racist underpinnings to task, and paved the way for a much deeper and more objective understanding of abolition and Reconstruction. Stampp's books detailed different forms of slave resistance in the South and argued that this resistance was largely responsible for bringing about abolition. This account posed a major challenge to the idea that black slaves were not politically conscious, a notion that Dunning and his followers used to justify white supremacy,* disenfranchisement,* and segregation.*

The Contemporary Debate

The idea that African Americans were biologically inferior to whites was widely accepted until the second half of the twentieth century. This view became dominant because social scientists such as Herbert Spencer* adapted nineteenth-century naturalist Charles Darwin's* research on evolutionary biology* and applied it—unscientifically—to racial difference. Spencer and other social scientists argued that black people were innately unintelligent and therefore unprepared and unfit for equal citizenship. Consequently, he defended slavery as an institution that was necessary to discipline and civilize blacks. This ideology, which served to justify exploitation and maintain the privileged position of whites in the United States, was also employed by European elites in countries such as Britain and France to justify colonialism* and the exploitation of foreign natural resources and manpower.

The Enlightenment* provided the intellectual context for ideas like this to emerge, and also to be challenged. Also known as the Age of Reason, this was a Western intellectual movement that aimed to question tradition and religious beliefs while advancing knowledge of the world through the scientific method. Although Du Bois and other scholars defied the feeble logic of the Dunning School prior to World War II, it is only since 1945 that it has been largely put to rest. The mass murder of Jewish people in the Holocaust* during World War II caused considerable reflection on claims that racial superiority has a biological basis; and the work of academics such as the influential anthropologist Franz Boas,* and a statement by the United Nations titled *The Race Question** (1950), undid assertions that racial superiority has any foundation in science, banishing these ideas from the mainstream.

MODULE 4
THE AUTHOR'S CONTRIBUTION

KEY POINTS

- Eric Foner's work is an example of historical revisionism,* which draws on fresh evidence and poses new questions to challenge traditional views of history.

- *Reconstruction* builds on previous revisionist histories to show that African Americans were the primary drivers of abolition* and the successes of the era; he attributes its failures to defiance and violence by the white Southern elite, and grave mistakes by the Northern government.

- In *Reconstruction,* Foner's analysis connects racism and economics, and places the perspectives of black slaves and freedmen at the heart of his study.

Author's Aims

The aim of Eric Foner's *Reconstruction: America's Unfinished Revolution, 1863–1877* is to present the social, political, and economic developments of Reconstruction, clearly detailing the great potential of the post-Civil War* era and analyzing the key players in its successes and failures. To achieve this, he leaves behind many assumptions embedded in the popular imagination and generates a compelling story through his analysis of an array of primary sources, including personal letters, debates in Congress,* and accounts of life on Southern plantations given by freedmen. Furthermore, as the social theorist W. E. B. Du Bois* had done 50 years earlier, Foner presents freed slaves "as the central actors in the drama of Reconstruction."[1]

Through much of the twentieth century, perceptions of this historical period were dominated by the interpretation offered by William A. Dunning* and his followers, who claimed that black

> ❝ Of the many questions raised by emancipation, none was more crucial to the future place of both blacks and whites in Southern society than how the region's economy would henceforth be organized. ❞
>
> Eric Foner, Reconstruction: *America's Unfinished Revolution, 1863–1877*

people were biologically inferior to whites, and that the failure of Reconstruction was evidence that black people were inherently incapable of handling freedom and democratic rights. This interpretation prevailed in popular thinking, providing a basis for racist practices and the widespread denial of civil rights* to black people. The views of the Dunning School* have since been discredited as racist nonsense, and revisionist historians, starting with W. E. B. Du Bois, have provided a truer picture of the possibilities, successes, and missed opportunities in this important part of America's past.

The historian Kenneth Stampp's* *The Peculiar Institution* (1956) and *The Era of Reconstruction, 1865–1877* (1965) are examples of revisionist works that influenced Foner's approach. Earlier social scientists like Herbert Spencer* and Ulrich Phillips*—influenced by the same racist logic that informed the Dunning School—had portrayed slavery as a social good, a generous system designed to discipline, civilize, and uplift black people, and to maintain peace between whites and blacks. Stampp, who was influenced by the civil rights movement* of the 1950s and 1960s, used vivid archival research to shatter these misconceptions, showing that slavery was a nightmarish exploitative system. He went further by demonstrating the determination and ingenuity with which black slaves resisted this system, and says that it was resistance by slaves themselves, rather than white benevolence, that ultimately defeated slavery.

Reconstruction follows in the revisionist tradition by detailing the central role African Americans played in shaping advances in American democracy. Rather than presenting emancipation* as an end point for black people, as portrayed in some previous works, Foner's study shows it as a stepping-stone to further struggles for greater freedom and equality.

Foner concludes that although Reconstruction never lived up to the ideals of the Radical Republicans,* there were nevertheless a number of valuable developments during this period. The most important of these being that, for the first time, many black people were allowed to become educated. Foner makes clear that positive developments such as this provided the context for the advances African Americans have made since.

Approach

Foner's approach to studying the American Civil War and Reconstruction is called historical revisionism,* as it challenges established interpretations of historical events. His method of research places African Americans (instead of whites) at the heart of his analysis, discovering new archival research, asking new questions, and drawing enhanced critical conclusions about the past.

Since the 1930s, revisionist works on Reconstruction have challenged representations of black people as innately inferior to whites and incapable of being productive in society. This view was not only present in the works of historians but in popular culture as well. For example, the filmmaker D. W. Griffith* directed *The Birth of a Nation* (1915), a popular film in which he portrayed black men as uncivilized, stupid, and sexually predatory toward white women. Furthermore, he presented the Ku Klux Klan* as an organization of heroes that would rescue the country from the threat to "white civilization" supposedly posed by black people. Historical revisionism has provided the world with credible and convincing counternarratives, effectively undermining the stereotypes they produce and reinforce in society. It does this by focusing on history from the bottom up, and paying particular attention to groups whose stories have often been ignored, such as women and ethnic minorities. Furthermore, it sees freedom and equality as concepts that are continually evolving.

The historian Michael Perman* praises Foner's *Reconstruction* as a work that "represents the mature revisionist perspective."[2] By this, he means that Foner's work is the culmination of a half-century of revisionist scholarship that has attempted to bury the racist underpinnings of the Dunning School.

Contribution in Context

Reconstruction builds on the work of Du Bois, Stampp, and other historical revisionists, to make a major contribution to the scholarly approach known as neo-abolitionism.* This is a term used in historiography* to describe those scholars who study African Americans within the context of the American Civil War and the Reconstruction era, and focuses on how black people transformed history, rather than merely portraying them as passive victims of exploitation.

Just as abolitionists once fought to free African Americans from slavery and obtain equal legal rights, since the 1950s neo-abolitionists have sought to advance equality in areas such as education, employment, and criminal justice by challenging racism based on false, stereotypical views of history.

Like Du Bois and Stampp, Foner shows a deep admiration for the abolitionists, and focuses much of his attention on how black activists shaped emancipation and major advances during Reconstruction, such as the Thirteenth,* Fourteenth,* and Fifteenth Amendments* to the US Constitution,* dealing with equal citizenship and voting rights for black men. However, as the title of Foner's book suggests, "America's revolution" remains "unfinished" because black people continue to struggle against racial discrimination and inequality today. In his view, researchers, teachers, journalists, and society as a whole need to make a continuous effort to improve our knowledge of these key periods in US history, and consider how past racism relates to inequalities that still persist.

NOTES

1   Eric Foner, *Reconstruction: America's Unfinished Revolution, 1863–1877* (New York: HarperCollins, 2014), xxix.

2   Michael Perman, "Eric Foner's Reconstruction: A Finished Revolution," *Reviews in American History* 17, no. 1 (1989): 73–8.

SECTION 2
IDEAS

MODULE 5
MAIN IDEAS

KEY POINTS

• Eric Foner's historical research illustrates the central role that African Americans played in accomplishing abolition* and the successes of Reconstruction.*

• Foner also shows how African Americans were not, as the racist interpretation of the Dunning School* had suggested, responsible for the failures of Reconstruction. Rather, he attributes these failures to Southern defiance and violence, and weak leadership by the Northern government after 1877.

• *Reconstruction* offers readers a clear analysis of one of the most important periods in American history, and draws a link between economic hardship and racial tensions.

Key Themes

Eric Foner's *Reconstruction: America's Unfinished Revolution, 1863–1877* presents a rigorous and compelling retelling of the period following the American Civil War* and the efforts to remake a united country without slavery. After the Northern* states' Union* Army, led by President Abraham Lincoln,* defeated the 11 Southern* Confederate* states that had attempted to secede* from the rest of the US, the country was left with the monumental task of reunifying and adjusting to a social structure in which all citizens were free and equal. Foner's research focuses on the role of African Americans in bringing about this victory and how their resistance efforts were central to the creation of Lincoln's Emancipation* Proclamation,* the legal act that marked the end of slavery in the United States.

The most significant leader in this movement was Frederick

> ❝ The fundamental underpinning of this interpretation was the conviction, to quote one member of the Dunning School, of 'negro incapacity.' The childlike blacks, these scholars insisted, were unprepared for freedom and incapable of properly exercising the political rights Northerners had thrust upon them. ❞
>
> Eric Foner, *Reconstruction: America's Unfinished Revolution, 1863–1877*

Douglass,* a former slave who escaped to the North, where his writings and speeches about the brutal reality of slavery inspired and fuelled the abolitionist cause. This reveals Foner's primary theme: the fact that African Americans were not passive victims of social ills or lucky beneficiaries of white generosity but, rather, the main drivers of these revolutionary social advancements. He goes on to highlight the profound effect that abolition had on American identity. For the first time, whites in the North and the South had to reflect on the fact that black people were formally equal citizens, and black people had to try to integrate into white society.

Reconstruction also presents an important exploration of the link between the aftermath of this bloody and divisive war and the challenges of reunification. Foner details the devastating economic and psychological effects of the war and abolition on the South, at the same time as the North enjoyed an unprecedented economic boom. The North attempted to extend its free labor ideology into the South in order to advance industrial capitalism* (the economic and social system dominant in the West today), but it was only partly successful, due to Southern defiance.

Although the measures put in place at the beginning of the Reconstruction period were abandoned too soon, and failed to provide a solid foundation for equal citizenship for African Americans, Foner asserts that there were several important successes and gains.

One notable example was the Freedmen's Bureau,* a federal government agency established to facilitate the transition from slavery to emancipation.

The key theme that runs through Foner's history is his focus on the crucial contributions by black people in the reshaping of American society, and that it was defiance by Southern whites, determined to resist racial equality, that undermined the potential opportunities of this pivotal historical period.

Exploring the Ideas

Foner starts by describing the radical impact that the Civil War had on the United States. The Confederacy, composed of 11 Southern states, seceded from the rest of the US because they wanted more power to rest in the hands of state-level government (including, but not limited to, the power to decide local policies on owning slaves), and less with the federal government. The Union side of the conflict wanted the country to remain intact. In 1863, midway through the Civil War, President Abraham Lincoln announced the Emancipation Proclamation. One of the great developments in American history, this order freed all slaves in the United States. As Northern troops advanced on Southern states, plantation owners abandoned their lands, and hundreds of thousands of emancipated slaves rushed to Union military camps, where they enlisted and fought for the North against their Southern oppressors.

The aftermath of the Civil War was greatly imbalanced. Following much destruction and bloodshed, the Confederate army surrendered in 1865; the North reclaimed the breakaway states and restructured their political, economic, and legal systems. The war destroyed Southern crops, plantations, and entire cities, while in the North the economy boomed, fostering resentment in the defeated South.

Lincoln's efforts to rebuild after the war involved some dramatic changes to America's political landscape. Important new legislation—

notably the Civil Rights Acts of 1866* and 1875,* and the Thirteenth,* Fourteenth,* and Fifteenth Amendments,* which together granted black people equal civil and political rights for the first time, and protection under the law—and institutions, particularly the Freedmen's Bureau, were put in place to consolidate the position of African Americans as full citizens. During this period, some black people were able to attend public schools and universities, and others who served in the Northern military during the war were able to stand for political office.

A number of Northerners traveled to the South to contribute to (and benefit from) these changes. So-called carpetbaggers* (who got their nickname from the inexpensive luggage they were said to have carried with them) were controversial because they stood for local elections having only lived in the South for a short time. While some people considered carpetbaggers progressives who wanted to contribute to important social changes, others viewed them as opportunists. The term scalawags* was also coined around this time, and referred to white Southerners who supported the abolitionist cause of the Republican Party of the day. Together, newly liberated African Americans and progressive white people, from both the North and the South, were helping to build a more equal society.

Unfortunately, all this was temporary. The defiance of Southern plantation owners and the violent, white supremacist Ku Klux Klan,* coupled with President Andrew Johnson's* lack of support for former slaves after Lincoln's death, ended the Reconstruction period in failure. Johnson returned Southern plantation lands confiscated by the Northern army to their original owners, rather than give them to freed slaves, and his policies showed little interest in achieving greater equality. Furthermore, using a variety of laws (for example, literacy tests and property-ownership requirements) and racist intimidation, Southern Democrats* were able to get around the new constitutional amendments and prevent newly enfranchised black people and many poor whites from voting. With so many of their opponents disenfranchised,* the Democrats won a majority of the seats in the House of Representatives* in the 1874 congressional election. This, coupled with the great depression of 1873, convinced President Rutherford B. Hayes* to remove Northern troops from the South in 1877, effectively bringing Reconstruction to an end, and allowing its phenomenal gains to slip away.

After the Northern withdrawal, about 80 percent of former slaves became sharecroppers* working for very little (and sometimes for no wages at all) on plantations owned by the same white farmers who had once been slave masters.

A set of laws called the Black Codes* imposed by the Southern States set back the gains of the Reconstruction even further. These laws prevented black people from exercising their right to freedom of speech and assembly, and criminalized unemployment and vagrancy* (that is, not having a settled home), making the exploitation of the sharecropping system the only option for former slaves unable to find other work. They also imposed voter qualifications (such as those mentioned above) to prevent black people from exercising their right to suffrage.* Finally, a conservative Supreme Court* decided on a number of cases that granted individual states power to limit the rights of African Americans, and effectively removed all of the legal gains they had received under the 1866 and 1875 Civil Rights Acts and the three new amendments to the Constitution.*

Language and Expression

Reconstruction is 690 pages long, and is packed with archival and historical detail. This can make for a difficult read, particularly for students or scholars unfamiliar with the basic themes of the Civil War and Reconstruction. That said, Foner explains these in a methodical and accessible way. He also defines all terms students might be unfamiliar with, such "carpetbaggers," "scalawags," and "sharecropping."

For those interested in a simpler analysis of the period, Foner has also published an abridged version of the text called *A Short History of Reconstruction* (1990). It essentially makes the same arguments, although targeted at an audience only seeking to learn the basics of the period.

Foner's use of the phrase "unfinished revolution" in the title of the work provides a hint of his perspective. Whereas early scholars of Reconstruction had represented abolition as an end point of the African American struggle, like other revisionists* Foner portrays the Emancipation Proclamation and the progressive reforms made during Reconstruction as a stepping-stone for the pursuit of greater freedom and equality. These fundamental democratic values that were promoted by America's Founding Fathers* (the thinkers and leaders who oversaw the young United States gain its independence from the British Empire) remain central to the struggle of African Americans and other minorities determined to realize these ideals.

MODULE 6
SECONDARY IDEAS

KEY POINTS

- Eric Foner's analysis of Reconstruction* highlights the struggle for economic resources and the huge disparity between Northern prosperity and Southern hardship following the Civil War.*

- The Freedmen's Bureau,* established in 1865, provided crucial services to former slaves. Although it was abandoned prematurely in 1877, it had a lasting effect on American democracy.

- Although the United States was founded on the ideals of freedom and equality, these founding principles are still not enjoyed by all Americans.

Other Ideas

Within Eric Foner's analysis of the post-Civil War period in *Reconstruction: America's Unfinished Revolution, 1863–1877*, the author also focuses on the economic disparities between the North and South, and exposes the specific ways in which the old establishment in the South worked to undermine the advances made by the Freedmen's Bureau, a federal government agency initiated by President Abraham Lincoln.* The objective of the Bureau was to help freed slaves integrate into Southern society during Reconstruction. It held classes to teach black people to read and write, set up public schools and universities, helped freed slaves reunite with their families, offered legal advice, and supported former slaves in finding employment.

Despite providing essential services, the Bureau lasted for only seven years. Andrew Johnson*—who became president after Lincoln's

> ❝ Long after the end of the Civil War, the experience
> of bondage remained deeply etched in blacks' collective
> memory. As one white writer noted years later, blacks
> could not be shaken from the conviction 'that the white
> race has barbarously oppressed them. ❞
>
> Eric Foner, *Reconstruction: America's Unfinished Revolution, 1863–1877*

assassination—was against prolonging it, claiming that it encroached on states' rights and prevented black people from becoming independent. Johnson, like other members of the white political elite, feared that helping black people achieve social equality would eventually lead them to try to gain an upper hand on whites over time. In 1872, due to the defiance of Southern plantation owners and Johnson's lack of support, President Ulysses S. Grant* (in office between 1869 and 1877) closed the agency.

Foner also casts a close critical eye on the economic benefits the North enjoyed in the years following the war, while the Southern economy and culture were almost ruined. For the North, the war was a profitable business for investors and industrialists, whereas for the South, it was devastating. Agricultural statistics from the period highlight that between 1860 and 1870, the value of farmland in the South fell by 50 percent; the number of horses and pigs decreased by 29 percent and 35 percent respectively; and agricultural production and profits decreased substantially.[1] In contrast, the war produced great prosperity in the North. Industry profits boomed, as did income from the stock market. By 1873, industrial production in the North had risen 75 percent compared to 1865 levels.[2]

Exploring the Ideas

According to Foner, the greatest success of the Freedmen's Bureau was its role in reuniting families and providing education. Prior to the

Civil War, nearly all black people were illiterate because they were prohibited from accessing public education and, in most states, it was illegal to teach slaves to read or write. Following emancipation,* freed slaves saw education as an essential part of the struggle against racism and exploitation. However, Southern plantation owners and politicians defiantly sought to restore the old system of oppression. In fact, just after the Freedmen's Bureau was established, Southern legislatures began passing the Black Codes,* laws that criminalized the movement and unemployment of African Americans, and limited their rights to freedom of speech and assembly.

By making unemployment and vagrancy* a crime within an environment where racism was rife, the majority of former slaves were pressured into sharecropping.* This system, established just after emancipation, allowed plantation owners to rent out a portion of their land. Their tenants were supposedly able to farm this land freely and benefit from their own harvest (except for any debts they had to pay). However, this changed due to reforms allowed by President Johnson in 1865, whereby black people became "employees" of plantation owners, meaning they lost their right to benefit from their own harvest. Under this revised system, they only received a portion of the harvest after plantation owners paid off debts and dividends to everyone else. In most cases, this meant that black people received nothing or little for their work, and since the Black Codes made it almost impossible for them to leave their jobs, they were entirely dependent on the plantation owners.

As Foner makes clear, slavery was first and foremost a system of labor exploitation. As Northern Union* troops entered Southern states,* plantation owners were forced to abandon their lands and, in the process, their slaves fled. Even after many regained their lands, there was total confusion as to how to rebuild the Southern economy. As Foner puts it, "Southern planters emerged from the Civil War in a state of shock. Their class had been devastated—physically, economically, and psychologically."[3] Intimidation and unfair labor laws such as those established in the Black Codes provided ways to effectively re-enslave much of the freed slave population.

Overlooked

As Foner convincingly shows, historical evidence supports the idea that Reconstruction failed to secure racial equality after the abolition of slavery, not because of a lack of political maturity or intelligence on the part of blacks, but because opportunities were sabotaged by the existing establishment. Nevertheless, the racist conclusions popularized by William A. Dunning* and his disciples (the Dunning School*) were deeply embedded in the popular understanding of Reconstruction. Revisionist* historians like W. E. B. Du Bois,* Kenneth Stampp,* and Eric Foner himself have made significant progress in uncovering the realities of the American Civil War and Reconstruction.

Despite the efforts of Foner's revisionist predecessors, and his own work as a prolific public intellectual, much more needs to be done to address the gap between the ideals of freedom and equality on which the US was founded, and the inequalities that persist to this day. Though the Dunning School has been thoroughly discredited, many textbooks continue to downplay the contributions of minorities shaping US history. Foner's approach encourages reflection on the paradox that America often claims to be an exceptional nation whose duty is to export enlightened democratic values globally; however, it often ignores the persistent racism and growing inequalities within its own borders. In this sense, the subtitle of the book, *America's Unfinished Revolution*, is highly significant. For Foner, the democratic values promoted by the Founding Fathers remain work in progress.

NOTES

1   Eric Foner, *Reconstruction: America's Unfinished Revolution, 1863–1877* (New York: HarperCollins, 2014), 125.

2   Foner, *Reconstruction*, 461.

3   Foner, *Reconstruction*, 129.

MODULE 7
ACHIEVEMENT

KEY POINTS

- Eric Foner has contributed to undermining the racist arguments of the Dunning School* that were the dominant perspective on the era of Reconstruction* until after World War II.*

- While conducting his research, Foner discovered 121 boxes of letters and other documents that gave him fresh insight into the experiences of Americans during the Reconstruction period.

- Foner's work has contributed to creating greater awareness of the central role African Americans played in shaping abolition* and the successes of Reconstruction.

Assessing the Argument

Eric Foner's objective when writing Reconstruction: *America's Unfinished Revolution, 1863–1877* "was to drive the final nail into the coffin of the Dunning School," exploding William A. Dunning's* argument that black people were simply incapable of meeting the responsibility that came with their liberation, offering instead "an alternative account of the era."[1] In this regard, it is the completion of half a century of revisionist* scholarship on the subject.

With this publication, he has largely put to rest the view that African Americans were responsible for the failures of Reconstruction because they were innately inferior, unprepared for freedom, and incapable of integrating into white society. This ideology, which reinforced stereotypes of black people as unintelligent, lazy, and dependent on whites, helped sustain the racial divisions and inequalities

> **❝** Once objective scholarship and modern experience
> rendered its racist assumptions untenable, familiar
> evidence read very differently, new questions suddenly
> came into prominence, and the entire edifice of the
> Dunning School had to fall. **❞**
>
> Eric Foner, *Reconstruction: America's Unfinished Revolution, 1863–1877*

of the Jim Crow* era—a time of legally enforced segregation that
only came to an end in the 1960s.

Foner does a masterful job of crafting a compelling account of
history that advances the earlier work of W. E. B. Du Bois,* Kenneth
Stampp,* and other historical revisionists. His original contribution
shows that Reconstruction was a struggle over economic resources, in
which the North sought to extend its free labor ideology, black people
struggled to gain economic autonomy, and Southern plantation
owners were determined to regain and protect their power and
privileges. He builds on previous revisionist works by portraying black
people as the key drivers of their own emancipation* and of much of
the progress the American South experienced from 1863 to 1877.

Achievement in Context

Since the United States became an independent nation in 1776,
American leaders from Thomas Jefferson* to Barack Obama* have
highlighted the country's core value of freedom. However, as Foner
shows in Reconstruction, this concept is often an empty or incomplete
promise. While the Declaration of Independence* and the
Constitution* of the United States, both founding documents,
emphasize the inalienable rights of life, liberty, and happiness, and
stress equality under the law, this is not always the reality for women,
African Americans, Native Americans, and other minorities. As the
author puts it, the history of American freedom "is a tale of debates,

disagreements, and struggles rather than a set of timeless categories or an evolutionary narrative toward a preordained goal."[2]

One of Foner's most significant achievements is his ability to show how America's minorities have played a crucial role historically in shaping the national concept of liberty: "It has been through battles at the boundaries of freedom—the efforts of racial minorities, women, workers, and other groups to secure freedom as they understood it— that the definition of freedom has been both deepened and transformed and the concept extended to realms for which it was not originally intended."[3]

Whereas President Abraham Lincoln* stated in 1863 in the speech known as the Gettysburg Address* that democracy means "government of the people, by the people, and for the people,"[4] interpretations have varied about who counted as "the people."

During the Civil War* and Reconstruction, slaves and freedmen insisted that they too were Americans, and therefore all boundaries limiting their freedom, equality, and ability to vote and run for government office should be abolished. The Fourteenth Amendment* to the US Constitution was a major step forward, giving black people equal protection under the law for the first time and allowing them to take their grievances to court—though in most cases they did not find justice. The Black Codes,* withdrawal of government support for the Freedmen's Bureau,* and other factors undermined the aims of Reconstruction and, as a result, this period was followed by another hundred years of racial oppression. However, as Foner shows, the progress made during the period of 1863–77 paved the way for many advances made since. In *Reconstruction* and other works, Foner makes clear that America's journey toward freedom is ongoing.

Limitations

Contemporary historians agree that *Reconstruction* is the most thorough and coherent account of the power struggles, successes, and failures of

Reconstruction, one of the most important and controversial eras in American history.

While Foner was able to discover previously unknown archival material to challenge the once-dominant Dunning School's interpretation of Reconstruction, his research was somewhat limited by the material and methods available before the existence of the Internet. Now, numerous resources on Reconstruction are readily available online, including congressional debates, court documents such as transcripts from Ku Klux Klan* hearings, plantation records, and nineteenth-century pamphlets and newspapers. Other scholars, such as the historian Steven Hahn,* author of *A Nation under Our Feet* (2003), have since discovered thousands of similar ("primary") sources that have provided further insight into the complexities of slavery, the Civil War, and Reconstruction.

Regardless of the limitations he faced during his research, Foner thoughtfully notes that "historical sources are only as useful as the questions historians ask of them."[5] Scholars agree that *Reconstruction* asks insightful questions and provides compelling answers. Historians continue to build on his revisionist account of Reconstruction, carrying on the tradition of thinkers committed to the core ideals of American society.

NOTES

1   Eric Foner, *Reconstruction: America's Unfinished Revolution, 1863–1877* (New York: HarperCollins, 2014), xxxi.

2   Eric Foner, *The Story of American Freedom* (New York: W. W. Norton, 1998), xiv.

3   Foner, *The Story of American Freedom*, xx.

4   Abraham Lincoln, "Gettysburg Address," November 19, 1863, accessed January 10, 2016, http://www.abrahamlincolnonline.org/lincoln/speeches/gettysburg.htm

5   Foner, *Reconstruction*, xxxiv.

MODULE 8
PLACE IN THE AUTHOR'S WORK

KEY POINTS

- *Reconstruction* has helped position Eric Foner as one of the most important contemporary historians of the American Civil War* and the leading contemporary expert on Reconstruction.*

- The text is the most comprehensive and detailed revisionist* account yet produced on the era of Reconstruction.

- Foner's body of work and his role as a public intellectual have played an important part in educating American society about the realities of the Civil War and Reconstruction.

Positioning

Although Eric Foner did not have significant experience in writing about Reconstruction when he embarked on the 13-year journey to produce *Reconstruction: America's Unfinished Revolution, 1863–1877*, he had completed a Bachelor of Arts and PhD in American history, writing his PhD dissertation on the rise of the Republican Party* (the largest right-wing party in the US), and the causes of the Civil War. Prior to publishing *Reconstruction* in 1988, Foner had published journal and press articles on Reconstruction and two books related to the subject: *Free Soil, Free Labor, Free Men* (1970) and *Nothing but Freedom: Emancipation and Its Legacy* (1983).

Free Soil, Free Labor, Free Men, which grew out of Foner's PhD dissertation, provided new insights into the causes of the Civil War. In it, he explains that the Republican Party believed that its ideology of

> **❝** From the enforcement of the rights of citizens to the stubborn problems of economic and racial injustice, the issues central to Reconstruction are as old as the American republic, and as contemporary as the inequalities that still afflict our society. **❞**
>
> Eric Foner, *Reconstruction: America's Unfinished Revolution, 1863–1877*

free labor (popular in the North) was superior to slave labor. He goes on to argue that while promoting the idea of free labor in the South was easy, implementing it was not. Ultimately, he describes the war as an ideological battle between Southerners, who saw slavery as the very basis of civilization, and Northerners, who considered it to be antidemocratic because it deprived individuals of education, basic labor rights, social mobility, the right to own property, and the right to take part in politics. Northerners also believed that paying workers a wage would make them more productive and therefore result in greater profit.[1]

Nothing But Freedom also changed the conventional understanding of US history. It presents an international perspective on themes such as freedom, labor, politics, power, and citizenship by comparing America's experience of Reconstruction with emancipation* and postemancipation developments in the British and French Caribbean, and Southern and Eastern Africa.[2]

Foner's 1983 article for *American Heritage* magazine, "The New View of Reconstruction,"[3] provides an overview of existing revisionist scholarship and sketches the basic arguments that he later covered in much greater detail in *Reconstruction*.

Integration

Since publishing *Reconstruction* in 1988, Foner has written or edited 15 books (at the time of writing), and has published numerous journal and press articles on different aspects of the Civil War, slavery, abolition, and Reconstruction. Recently, he has focused on the life, personality, successes, and failures of President Abraham Lincoln* (who, in delivering the Emancipation Proclamation★ in 1863, formally ended slavery) in *Our Lincoln: New Perspectives on Lincoln and His World* (2008) and *The Fiery Trial: Abraham Lincoln and American Slavery* (2010).

In addition to his writing, Foner has curated several important historical exhibitions. One of these, "America's Reconstruction," was held at the Virginia Historical Society in Richmond, and was later reproduced in several other cities across the US, including New York and Chicago. He has served as an advisor for the first Public Broadcasting Service (PBS) television series on Reconstruction, published a free online lecture series on the Civil War and Reconstruction through Columbia University, and appears frequently as a commentator in the press. Through both his scholarly contributions and his role as a public intellectual and activist, Foner has made a significant impact on the popular understanding of American history from 1863 to 1877, and its relationship to contemporary race relations.

Significance

Scholars agree that *Reconstruction* is the most comprehensive revisionist account produced to date of the period from 1863 to 1877. It overturned the idea that African Americans were responsible for the failures of Reconstruction, and has highlighted the extent to which emancipated men and women shaped nineteenth-century American history and democracy.

Foner is one of only two people to have served as president of the three most important professional organizations in the field of history—the Organization of American Historians, the American Historical Association, and the Society of American Historians—and one of only a small number of historians to have won the Bancroft and Pulitzer Prizes in the same year, both signs of the prestigious position he holds in his profession.

The eminent historian Steven Hahn* of the University of Pennsylvania is unreserved in his praise of Foner: "Like his mentor Richard Hofstadter,* he has had an enormous influence on how other historians, as well as a good cut of the general reading public, have come to think about American history ... Indeed, when one considers the chronological and topical range of Foner's many books and essays—not to mention those of his doctoral students—only Hofstadter, C. Vann Woodward,* David Brion Davis,* and, in an earlier era, Charles Beard* (who was also at Columbia) would seem to be his genuine rivals in impact and accomplishment."[4]

NOTES

1   Eric Foner, *Free Soil, Free Labor, Free Men* (New York: Oxford University Press, 1995).

2   Eric Foner, *Nothing but Freedom: Emancipation and Its Legacy* (Baton Rouge, LA: Louisiana State University Press, 1983).

3   Eric Foner, "The New View of Reconstruction," *American Heritage* 34, no. 6 (1983).

4   Steven Hahn, "The Other American Revolution: A Book Review of *Forever Free: The Story of Emancipation and Reconstruction* by Eric Foner," *New Republic Online*, accessed January 10, 2016, http://inside.sfuhs.org/dept/history/US_History_reader/Chapter6/reviewoffoner.htm

SECTION 3
IMPACT

MODULE 9
THE FIRST RESPONSES

KEY POINTS

- Some historians have noted that although Eric Foner presented numerous factors that led to the failure of Reconstruction,* he failed to clearly identify which he thought were the most important.

- Other critics felt that *Reconstruction* focused only on the American North and South without acknowledging how the events of this period related to the westward expansion of the United States.

- Foner has not responded directly to these criticisms. Rather, his focus has shifted to better understanding the concepts of freedom and exceptionalism* in American history, and the life and legacy of Abraham Lincoln.* ("Exceptionalism" refers to the notion that something is inherently exceptional—a special, unique case.)

Criticism

Although there is an academic consensus that Eric Foner's *Reconstruction: America's Unfinished Revolution, 1863–1877* is an unrivaled revisionist* analysis of the period, certain historians have criticized aspects of the book.

In one review, the historian Michael Perman* argues that Foner did not adequately explain the reasons why Reconstruction failed: "The reader may finish the book and still be left wondering exactly why Reconstruction did not work out—so many problems and difficulties arose to undermine it—and all are discussed—that it becomes difficult to assign priority or relative significance among all these contributory elements."[1]

❝ Rather than passive victims of the actions of others or simply a 'problem' confronting white society, blacks were active agents in the making of Reconstruction. **❞**

Eric Foner, *Reconstruction: America's Unfinished Revolution, 1863–1877*

Another scholar, Heather Cox Richardson,* argues in *West from Appomattox* (2007) that Foner and other historians of Reconstruction should not limit their analysis to the American North and South. She points out that Reconstruction radically transformed the entire country.[2] Due to large-scale immigration, rapid industrialization, and the construction of railways and other new infrastructure, the United States experienced great westward expansion in the late nineteenth century. Together, Southerners, Northerners, and Westerners developed a national identity and made America into a major power. Westward expansion helped establish the American middle class, and extended the concepts of free labor, individualism, and social mobility through hard work.

Responses

Foner has never responded directly to Perman's minor criticism that *Reconstruction* does not put forward a clear hierarchy of reasons why Reconstruction failed. In later works, such as *A Short History of Reconstruction*, Foner continues to portray a combination of numerous factors that undermined Reconstruction. The factors Foner identifies all center around the desire on the part of the white Southern elite to regain and protect their privilege, and the lack of political will in the administrations that followed the death of Abraham Lincoln, president during the Civil War,* to properly stand up to this pressure.

Similarly, Foner never directly responds to Richardson. However, in *Reconstruction* and some of his subsequent work, he does acknowledge generally that immigration, industrialization, the construction of railroads and other infrastructure, and westward expansion, shaped a new concept of American national identity. That said, Foner's primary interest and emphasis is the North and the South, and he has not sought to address the Western US in any significant detail. Recently, his attention has turned largely to understanding how the concepts of freedom and American exceptionalism (the idea that America is unique among nations) have developed over time, analyzing the successes and shortcomings of these ideas. He has also engaged in detailed research into the life and legacy of Abraham Lincoln.

Conflict and Consensus

There is now an overwhelming consensus among historians in disregarding the conclusions of the Dunning School;* and revisionist histories of the Civil War and Reconstruction period are universally accepted. Historians in the revisionist tradition continue to shed light on the details of different aspects of Civil War and Reconstruction-era history.

Steven Hahn's* *A Nation under Our Feet* (2003) details the evolution of nineteenth-century black political participation following the mass migration of African Americans from the South to the North. The notable historian Nicholas Lemann's* Redemption: *The Last Battle of the Civil War* (2006) focuses on the violent overthrow of Reconstruction in Mississippi, where armed whites effectively murdered any black people who resisted their rule. Locating his study in the former slave state of South Carolina, the historian Bruce Baker's* *What Reconstruction Meant* (2007) illuminates the differences between the African American collective memory of Reconstruction as a time of hope whose lessons could fuel further struggles into the twentieth century, and that of South Carolina's whites who largely remembered Reconstruction as an era of destruction and suffering.

Heather Cox Richardson's *West from Appomattox* emphasizes the importance of westward expansion during the period of Reconstruction. Arguing that, in some cases, freedmen faced worse conditions than slaves, the historian Stephen Budiansky's* *The Bloody Shirt* (2008) recounts the brutal attacks on black people during Reconstruction by the Ku Klux Klan* and other white supremacists who were deeply embittered by the result of the Civil War and the abolition of slavery.

While all of these historical revisionist accounts have enhanced our understanding of one of the most complex and controversial periods in American history, Foner's *Reconstruction* is widely regarded as the most significant contribution.

NOTES

1   Michael Perman, "Eric Foner's Reconstruction: A Finished Revolution," *Reviews in American History* 17, no. 1 (1989): 73–8.

2   Heather Cox Richardson, *West from Appomattox: The Reconstruction of America after the Civil War* (New Haven, CT: Yale University Press, 2007).

MODULE 10
THE EVOLVING DEBATE

KEY POINTS

- Eric Foner has greatly enhanced our understanding of Reconstruction,* and in particular the central role of African Americans in bringing about emancipation* and further progress from 1863 to 1877.

- *Reconstruction* is an example of historical revisionism* because it challenges dominant interpretations of historical events.

- Today, historical revisionists continue to offer new perspectives on the American Civil War* and Reconstruction, as they discover new primary sources and ask new questions.

Uses and Problems

Eric Foner's *Reconstruction: America's Unfinished Revolution, 1863–1877* is widely considered to be the most thorough and coherent account of the Reconstruction period following the Civil War. Besides his scholarly writing, Foner is a prolific public intellectual and civil rights* activist. He frequently writes in the press and speaks on television, and has organized several public historical exhibitions.

Foner's work is still of particular relevance because, while freedom and equality are the founding values of the United States, in practice, African Americans continue to face discrimination and inequalities in areas such as education, employment, and criminal justice.

A recent rash of allegations of racially motivated police violence serve as evidence that institutional oppression of African Americans is an ongoing struggle, sparking uprisings like the Baltimore Riots*

❝ Who owns history? Everyone and no one—which is why the study of the past is a constantly evolving, never-ending journey of discovery. **❞**

Eric Foner, *Who Owns History? Rethinking the Past in a Changing World*

(which followed the death of Freddie Gray,* a 25-year-old black man, while in police custody in 2015) and the influential Black Lives Matter* activist campaign. These events and others have provoked public statements from President Barack Obama* on civil rights and have triggered some reforms of the criminal justice system. Politicians such as the Democratic* politician Bernie Sanders* have also attracted further attention to the links between racism and economic deprivation.

The underlying questions in *Reconstruction* and many of Foner's other works on US history have strong ties to themes that remain relevant today. Foner asks us to reflect on: what citizenship means and who has access to it, majority and minority rights, the power relationship between states and the federal government, and the relationship between terrorism (by white supremacist groups like the Ku Klux Klan* in the past, and present-day radical extremists) and the protection of freedom and civil liberties.

Schools of Thought

Foner's work is perhaps best understood in the context of historiography*—the evolution of a historical debate and the various approaches to a particular topic or historical period. Historiography acknowledges that history is not simply a body of objective facts or fixed information, but rather that our understanding of history is constantly changing as new evidence comes to light or as dominant perspectives shift.

Revisionism is an approach that challenges traditional

interpretations of history. It does so by rigorously scrutinizing orthodox claims and focusing on the voices of historically marginalized groups, such as women and ethnic minorities. In the case of Reconstruction, a half century of revisionist historians have shown the previously dominant interpretation of Reconstruction, offered by the Dunning School,* to be invalid and have advanced our understanding of the great complexities of the Civil War and Reconstruction. Their works have focused on firsthand accounts of black people during that era, and through this we have found that, contrary to the conclusions of Dunning School historiography, they were not simply passive victims of discrimination. Black intellectuals such as Frederick Douglass* and W. E. B. Du Bois* started this process, and scholars such as Foner and Stephen Hahn* have continued it.

Together, these intellectuals have discredited the view that white people were responsible for the successes of Reconstruction and black people for its failures. Since the publication of *Reconstruction*, scholars like Hahn have discovered new sources of information and have continued to ask nuanced questions to offer further insights into key aspects of the period.

In Current Scholarship

Steven Hahn's *A Nation under Our Feet* (2003) is an important revisionist contribution to the subject. Hahn starts by detailing how black people forged a degree of labor independence during the late stage of slavery. He then explains different ways in which slaves resisted oppression, including strikes, acts of sabotage, and even violent rebellion against slave masters. From there, he moves on to the era of emancipation, when black people fled abandoned plantations during the Civil War and rushed to Union* lines to join the struggle against the South. During this period, African Americans also began forming black associations and churches to organize in the struggle against racism and violence. Hahn emphasizes the importance of religion as a source of strength and nonviolent resistance. After achieving civil rights under the Thirteenth,* Fourteenth,* and Fifteenth Amendments,* black people gradually made progress in education and politics.[1]

Another important revisionist work is Bruce Baker's* *What Reconstruction Meant* (2007). Baker shows how white South Carolinians portrayed Reconstruction as a dark time for the South, an era when the North destroyed its economy and way of life. This bitter ideology served as a justification for segregation* in public accommodations and other injustices under the Jim Crow laws.[2]

These two revisionist accounts, among many others, have built on the work of Foner and the historians who came before him, and have greatly enhanced our understanding of Reconstruction.

NOTES

1   Steve Hahn, *A Nation under Our Feet* (Cambridge, MA: Belknap Press, 2003).

2   Bruce Baker, *What Reconstruction Meant* (Charlottesville, VA: University of Virginia, 2007).

MODULE 11
IMPACT AND INFLUENCE TODAY

KEY POINTS

- *Reconstruction* may be thought the most significant revisionist* account produced to date on the Reconstruction.*

- Revisionist scholars have discredited the racist conclusions of the once-dominant Dunning School,* and future scholars are likely to keep expanding our knowledge of this period.

- Many of Foner's key themes—among them freedom and equality, terrorism, and the relationship between state and federal government power—remain highly relevant today.

Position

Eric Foner's *Reconstruction: America's Unfinished Revolution, 1863–1877* is widely considered to be the most influential historical account produced to date on this period. Scholars such as Michael Perman* see it as the culmination of 50 years of revisionist scholarship on the subject. Furthermore, Foner's research, teaching, press articles, television appearances, and public exhibitions have helped his ideas reach a wide audience beyond academic circles.

Today, as a result of the hard work of revisionists, outdated views of the supposed benefits of slavery and the myth that black people have been passive throughout American history have been put to rest, and the full horrors of slavery and institutional racism are universally recognized. Unfortunately, these problems are not yet relegated to the past, and minorities continue to struggle against discrimination and inequality. For this reason, Foner's work remains relevant, not only to

> **❝** Foner has established himself as the leading authority on the Reconstruction period ... This book is not simply a distillation of the secondary literature; it is a masterly account—broad in scope as well as rich in detail and insight. **❞**
>
> Michael Perman, "Eric Foner's Reconstruction: A Finished Revolution"

academic debate, but to society at large.

For Foner, racism is alive and well in contemporary America and, even in mundane forms, it must be recognized and opposed. He recently wrote, "The face of racism, to me, today is a guy in a three-piece suit, a banker at Wells Fargo, for example, who is pushing black people into subprime mortgages [i.e. high interest rate mortgages for poor people with bad credit], and they're going to lose their house, whereas a white person with exactly the same financial record is going into a better mortgage. So, you know, there is racism built into all sorts of institutions. Often it's not quite as visible. But that's part of what it means to analyze society, to see through the facade and see what's really, you know, in the depths of the society."[1]

Interaction

W. E. B. Du Bois's* book *Black Reconstruction in America* (1935) was the first major revisionist history of the Reconstruction. His final chapter, "The Propaganda of History," describes the prejudiced misinformation presented by William A. Dunning* and advocates of his school of thought. Du Bois convincingly exposes the magnitude of racist accounts of US history: "In propaganda against the Negro since emancipation* in this land, we face one of the most stupendous efforts the world ever saw to discredit human beings, an effort involving universities, history, science, social life, and religion."[2]

Dunning's perspective, together with popular culture, such as the

1915 film *Birth of a Nation* and Claude Bowers's* 1929 best-selling book *The Tragic Era,* helped create an academic and mainstream perception that justified and sustained black disenfranchisement* and racial segregation.*

While the residue of this perspective can still be found in society, half a century of revisionist historians have made a monumental effort to put it to rest by detailing the realities of slavery and Reconstruction, revealing the central role that African Americans have played in advancing American democracy. And although Foner has been a very important part of this, he insists that there remains much ignorance in society about Reconstruction, and that the work of revisionists must continue to educate the public. As he puts it, "The main thing is that people know next to nothing about Reconstruction. And what they do know is just not correct. I mean, just basic myths. People say, 'They gave the right to vote to blacks but they disenfranchised all the whites.' Well, that's completely untrue … but people think that's a known fact."[3]

The Continuing Debate

Research on the American Civil War* and the era of Reconstruction has flourished in recent years, with scholars finding important new angles from which to study this decisive time. Scholars like the African American studies professor Thavolia Glymph* have shifted the focus away from men as the only major historical players, and have concentrated on the intersections between gender, race, labor, and politics. Her book *Out of the House of Bondage: The Transformation of the Plantation Household* (2008) examines the ways in which black women resisted racism during slavery and Reconstruction, and how Southern white women reacted to this in an attempt to maintain their power and privileges.

Another important area of recent research involves drawing meaningful comparisons between the end of slavery and Reconstruction in the United States, with abolition and its aftermath in former British and French colonies. Studies such as that of the historian Demetrius Eudell's* *Political Languages of Emancipation in the British Caribbean and the U.S. South* (2002) focus on the need to better understand how developments in one context relate to and influence others by comparing developments in South Carolina and Jamaica.

Other scholars of Reconstruction have extended their focus beyond the period of 1863 to 1877. Stephen Hahn's *A Nation under Our Feet* (2003) locates the seeds of emancipation in different forms of political resistance during slavery, and he extends his inquiry into the twentieth century, in order to better understand disenfranchisement and successful examples of black political participation.

The historian Stephen Budiansky's* *The Bloody Shirt* (2008) is just one example of a study that focuses on the ways in which the Ku Klux Klan* and other white supremacist* groups terrorized black people during Reconstruction. Here, Budiansky highlights the way terrorism can dictate politics. The federal government used a combination of laws, intelligence, and troops to combat these groups, before eventually pulling its troops out of the South in 1877, and to a certain extent turning a blind eye to their violence. Historians like Foner and Budiansky have made further links between white supremacist terror during Reconstruction and contemporary extremist violence, seeking better ways to understand this phenomenon and effective methods to combat it.

NOTES

1   Amy Goodman and Juan González, "Civil War Historian Eric Foner on the Radical Possibilities of Reconstruction," *Democracy Now*, March 11, 2015, accessed December 9, 2015, http://www.democracynow.org/blog/2015/3/11/civil_war_historian_eric_foner_on

2   W. E. B. Du Bois, *Black Reconstruction in America* (London: Transaction Publishers, 2013), 649.

3   Goodman and González, "Civil War Historian Eric Foner."

MODULE 12
WHERE NEXT?

KEY POINTS

- *Reconstruction* has become a classic work, presenting a clear and compelling account of the end of the American Civil War* and the era that followed it.

- Foner's approach places African Americans at the center of his historical account and gives them the credit they deserve for the important contributions they made to American democracy.

- *Reconstruction* has changed the way we see and teach American history, and it will likely continue to be a major reference point in and outside of academia.

Potential

In the introduction to *Reconstruction: America's Unfinished Revolution, 1863–1877*, Eric Foner situates his research among the fundamental questions about the American national identity: "Citizenship, rights, freedom, democracy—as long as these questions remain central to our society, so too will the necessity of an accurate understanding of Reconstruction."*[1]

Foner's impressive body of work represents a new approach and a fresh set of questions. In this way, he moves beyond previous revisionist* work to enhance our understanding of the past and how it relates to present-day examples of racism and inequality.

Although legalized slavery is a thing of the past and progress been made in American democracy and race relations since Reconstruction, including the election of Barack Obama* as the first black president in 2009, racism persists, and African Americans and other minorities

> **❝In a global age, the forever-unfinished story of American freedom must become a conversation with the entire world, not a complacent monologue with ourselves.❞**
> Eric Foner, "American Freedom in a Global Age"

continue to face discrimination. Recognizing both how far the US has come, and how far it still has to go, Foner's work urges us to seek a more sophisticated understanding of racism, particularly the influence of economics on racism and how race intersects with class. He points out that deindustrialization (the process by which industry ceases to provide employment and to contribute to a region or a nation's economy) has had a major impact on working-class African Americans, and black people face unemployment rates that are double those of white Americans.[2] The incarceration rate for black people is six times higher than for white people.[3] These stark facts illustrate the enduring importance of Foner's work. Although the nature of racism has changed, it continues to be a major social problem.

Future Directions

In the future, scholars will continue to discover new primary sources and ask novel questions about key periods in American history such as the Civil War and Reconstruction. As they do so, more critical interpretations will likely emerge. Because of the work of scholars such as W. E. B. Du Bois,* Kenneth Stampp,* and Foner, since the 1960s historically marginalized groups have been much more represented in scholarly literature, and traditional views have undergone major revisions.

One aspect of Reconstruction that could attract further attention is the relationship between the experiences of African Americans in the South and those of Hispanic immigrants in the Southwest,

Chinese immigrants on the West Coast, and Native Americans in different parts of the United States. From 1863 to 1877, the entire country, not just the North and South, was under Reconstruction. For example, America purchased and integrated Alaska in 1867. All of these minorities—and others—have helped redefine freedom, citizenship, identity, and democracy in the American context.

Another element of Foner's work that could also attract further attention relates to the ideological origins of American imperialism*— the policy of empire-building through military, political, economic, or cultural means. Foner suggests that this began in the last quarter of the nineteenth century and was related to the view, in which the evolutionary theories of the naturalist Charles Darwin* were misapplied to society, that nonwhites could not govern themselves ("social Darwinism"*), and that the United States was an exceptional nation that ought to spread its founding values of freedom and equality abroad (a concept known as American exceptionalism*). Foner makes clear that, while freedom and equality have been a common doctrine of American political administrations over time, these elements have always excluded certain groups, such as women and African Americans during Reconstruction.

In *Reconstruction,* Eric Foner does not just offer a new account of this historical period. He also reflects on the major philosophical and social foundations of American life: the meaning of freedom and equality changing over time, citizenship and shifting perceptions of who should be able to access it, the relationship between majority and minority rights, the relationship between the states and the federal government, and terrorism and approaches to overcoming it. All of these issues continue to evolve and present challenges, as well as opportunities, in contemporary life.

Summary

Eric Foner's *Reconstruction: America's Unfinished Revolution, 1863–1877* is widely considered to be the most important and substantial revisionist account to date of the changes and challenges following the American Civil War. Following in the footsteps of the social theorist W. E. B. Du Bois 50 years before him, Foner represents freed slaves "as the central actors in the drama of Reconstruction."[4] To demonstrate this, he presents evidence from a wide range of primary sources, ranging from firsthand accounts of struggles on plantations to transcripts of congressional debates and legal trials.

While Foner concludes that Reconstruction ultimately failed because of the defiance of Southern plantation owners, the violence of white supremacist* groups, and the poor leadership of presidents after Abraham Lincoln,* he shows that this period was a remarkable experiment in interracial democracy built quickly from the ashes of slavery, and an era in which African Americans achieved many important, albeit temporary, advances. He also argues that these struggles provided the context for the progress African Americans have made since.

Foner's account is a major contribution to a half century of revisionist works that together have largely discredited the racist interpretations of the Dunning School* that, until the 1960s, provided the dominant readings of Reconstruction. While the residue of this school of thought still exists to some extent in the popular imagination, Foner and other revisionists have worked hard to detail the realities of Reconstruction, and to emphasize that African Americans were major subjects of American history rather than mere objects of racism, segregation, and exploitation.

Reconstruction is a landmark text in its field, and one that has greatly enhanced our understanding of the period from 1863 to 1877. Along with Foner's wider body of work, it has positioned him as the leading contemporary expert on the subject.

NOTES

1   Eric Foner, *Reconstruction: America's Unfinished Revolution, 1863–1877* (New York: HarperCollins, 2014), xLII.

2   Neil Irwin, Claire Cain Miller, and Margot Sanger-Katz, "America's Racial Divide, Chartered," *New York Times*, August 19, 2014, accessed January 10, 2015, http://www.nytimes.com/2014/08/20/upshot/americas-racial-divide-charted.html?_r=0

3   George Gao, "Chart of the Week: The Black–White Gap in Incarceration Rates," *Pew Research Center*, July 18, 2014, accessed January 10, 2015, http://www.pewresearch.org/fact-tank/2014/07/18/chart-of-the-week-the-black-white-gap-in-incarceration-rates/

4   Foner, *Reconstruction*, xxIx.

GLOSSARY

GLOSSARY OF TERMS

Abolitionists: those who fought to end slavery in the United States and elsewhere.

American Civil War: a war fought in the United States between Northern (Union) and Southern (Confederate) states between 1861 and 1865 over the Southern states' desire to politically withdraw from the Union and govern themselves; in this desire, the right to hold slaves, among other economic issues, was particularly important.

Baltimore Riots: a series of protests that took place in Baltimore, Maryland, in April 2015 in response to police violence toward African Americans. The injury and subsequent death of Freddie Gray, a 25-year-old black man, at the hands of police sparked the uprising.

Bancroft Prize: an award for books on diplomacy or American history, presented annually by the trustees of Columbia University.

Black Codes: laws passed by Southern states in 1865 and 1866 that restored white supremacy in the South after emancipation. Under these codes, the basic civil rights of black people were severely limited. The Black Codes served as the precursors for the Jim Crow segregation laws, eventually repealed in the mid-1960s.

Black Lives Matter: an activist movement, formed in 2013 in response to police shootings of African Americans, that campaigns for police accountability and reform of the US criminal justice system.

British Empire: a former empire of countries under the control of Great Britain. At its peak, it encompassed roughly one-quarter of the earth's surface.

Capitalism: an economic system based on private ownership, private enterprise, and the maximization of profit.

Carpetbaggers: a derogatory name that refers to Northerners who moved to the South after the American Civil War.

Civil rights: those rights legally granted by a society to all individuals who constitute that society. These can be distinguished from natural rights that, according to the Anglo-American political thinker Thomas Paine, are those rights to which all human beings are entitled by virtue of their existence.

Civil Rights Act of 1866: this Act granted black men the same rights as white men. In theory, this protected all citizens against discrimination on the grounds of race or previous status as a slave.

Civil Rights Act of 1875: this Act granted black people equal treatment in public places, including transportation.

Civil Rights Movement: the period of the 1950s and 1960s when black people in the United States struggled against discrimination and for greater equality.

Colonialism: the policy followed by a nation or people that takes full or partial political control over another country and occupies it. It often involves the economic exploitation of the colonies and colonized people.

Confederate States of America: the group of seven slave states that split from the United States in 1861. This event led to the American Civil War.

Congress: the legislative body of the US federal government. It consists of two houses: the lower chamber (the House of Representatives) and the upper chamber (the Senate).

Constitution (of the United States of America): a document adopted in 1787 and ratified in 1789 that acts as the supreme law of the United States. It outlines the civil rights and liberties afforded to citizens; deems unconstitutional any attempts by the states to nullify its laws; and details a system of checks and balances between the three main branches of government: the executive, the legislative, and the judicial.

Crisis **magazine (or** *The Crisis*)**:** cofounded by the sociologist W. E. B. Du Bois in 1910, this is the official magazine of the National Association for the Advancement of Colored People (NAACP).

Declaration of Independence: the document written by the American revolutionaries declaring their intention to create a new state and listing their grievances against the British government.

Democracy: a system of government in which citizens are able to participate in the decision-making process of their government, usually through electing representatives. In some places and historical periods, full access to the democratic process has been limited, excluding women, certain ethnic groups, and people who do not own land, among other examples.

Democratic Party: during the Civil War and Reconstruction, the Democrats were the more conservative of the two main parties and favored allowing each state to decide its own laws on slavery rather than supporting national abolition. The Southern Democrats were a faction of the Democratic Party particularly opposed to granting rights to black Americans.

Disenfranchisement: the removal of voting rights, or the prevention of individuals or groups of people from exercising these rights

Dunning School (of Reconstruction): the dominant interpretation of Reconstruction until the civil rights movement of the 1960s. The historian William A. Dunning and his followers argued that granting black people the right to vote and hold office was a serious error because they were unprepared for and incapable of meeting such responsibility.

Emancipation: the act of freeing someone from slavery or other kinds of bondage or oppression.

Emancipation Proclamation: an act issued by Abraham Lincoln in 1863 in the midst of the American Civil War that made slavery illegal in the United States.

Enlightenment: an early modern (seventeenth- and eighteenth-century) cultural, intellectual, and philosophical movement that emphasized social and personal progress through education, science, individualism, and reason.

Evolutionary biology: a subdiscipline of biology concerned with the evolution of life on earth. It is commonly associated with English naturalist Charles Darwin.

Exceptionalism: the sense of someone or something as special, unique, or particularly distinct in its category.

Fifteenth Amendment (1870): the Amendment to the

Constitution of the United States that granted all black males the right to vote; it removed any discrimination on the grounds of race or previous status as a slave.

Founding Fathers of the United States of America: the individuals from the 13 North American colonies of Britain who led the Revolution and established the United States. The term is also used more narrowly to describe those who either signed the 1776 Declaration of Independence or those who helped draft the Constitution in 1787.

Fourteenth Amendment (1868): the Amendment to the Constitution of the United States that granted black men (former slaves) citizenship and equal rights.

Freedmen's Bureau: a federal government agency that existed from 1865 to 1877. It was initiated by Abraham Lincoln and closed by Ulysses S. Grant; its purpose was to aid the integration of freed slaves into American society during Reconstruction.

Free labor ideology: the economic system promoted by the North during the American Civil War. It stressed that all individuals should have basic labor rights, including the right to leave a job, and to be able to own and accumulate property.

Gettysburg Address: a famous speech delivered by President Abraham Lincoln on November 19, 1863. In it, he described the Civil War as an event fought in defense of democracy, national unity, and equality (the abolition of slavery).

Great depression of 1873: an economic depression in Europe and the United States from 1873 to 1879. During this period, many argued that black people were responsible for the crisis and failure of Reconstruction; this argument helped justify the segregationist laws that defined the Jim Crow period (from the late nineteenth to the mid-twentieth centuries).

Historiography: the study of how history is researched and written, and the idea that perspectives on history are always evolving.

Holocaust: the genocide of Jews and other minorities in Europe by the German Nazi Party during World War II.

House of Representatives: a legislative chamber of the United States Congress; the other is the Senate.

Imperialism: the extension of a nation's influence by territorial acquisition or by the establishment of political, cultural, or economic dominance over other nations.

Jim Crow: a set of laws passed in the post-Reconstruction period, mostly by Southern states, that established and reinforced racial segregation in public places.

Ku Klux Klan: a white supremacist group, founded in 1866, that terrorized black people in the South, and demanded the restoration of slavery.

Lincoln Prize: an honor awarded by Gettysburg College for the best scholarly work about Abraham Lincoln.

National Association for the Advancement of Colored People (NAACP): a black civil rights organization co-founded by the social theorist W. E. B. Du Bois in 1909 that works to end racism and achieve equality.

Neo-abolitionism: a term used in historiography to describe scholars who study African Americans within the context of slavery, the American Civil War, and the Reconstruction era, and focus on how these individuals transformed history, rather than merely seeing them as victims.

Northern states: the non-slave-holding states that did not secede from the United States during the Civil War.

Pulitzer Prize: a highly coveted award for excellence in writing.

The Race Question: one of four documents produced by the United Nations cultural body UNESCO that sought to clarify the concept of "race" and condemn racism in the aftermath of the Holocaust.

Radical: a person who advocates drastic political, economic, or social reform.

Radical Reconstruction: reforms in favor of African Americans that took place from 1863 to 1877.

Radical Republicans: a faction of the Republican Party from around 1854 to 1877 who advocated an end to slavery and equal rights for African Americans.

Reconstruction: the period from 1865 to 1877 when the federal government of the United States reincorporated the Southern states into the Union. During Reconstruction, Southern states were militarily occupied and administered by federal officials. While African Americans made important progress in terms of freedom and equality, the segregationist laws of the Jim Crow period, in operation between the late nineteenth and the mid-twentieth centuries, overturned these advances.

Republican Party: a party that emerged in 1854 and defended the preservation of the United States against Southern secession and an end to slavery.

Revisionism: a scholarly movement that questions orthodox interpretations of history. Since the 1930s, revisionist historians of nineteenth-century America have sought to account for the realities of Reconstruction and in the process discredit the racist readings of the Dunning School.

Scalawags: a derogatory name for white Southerners who supported the federal government during Reconstruction.

Secession: the political act of withdrawing from a federation. In this case, it refers to the Southern states that seceded from the United States to form the Confederate States of America, which sparked the American Civil War.

Segregation: the legally enforced separation of people of different ethnicities, religions, sex, and so on.

Sharecropping: the labor system on plantations that replaced slavery after 1863. Plantation owners (mostly former slave masters) rented land to freed slaves (and some poor whites) in exchange for a share of the harvest. However, plantation owners also provided seed, equipment, and other essentials, trapping former slaves in a level of debt that meant they worked for very little or nothing at all, just as they had under slavery.

Social Darwinism: the adaptation and misapplication of the ideas of the English naturalist Charles Darwin regarding evolutionary biology to the social sciences. Herbert Spencer and other sociologists used this to argue that whites were naturally superior to nonwhites.

Southern Democrats: the conservative Democratic Party in the Southern states who defended slavery.

Southern states: the American states whose economies were primarily based on slave labor and large-scale agricultural plantations.

Suffrage: the right to vote. In 1870, the Fifteenth Amendment to the Constitution of the United States granted black males this right. Women only won suffrage in 1920 (the Nineteenth Amendment), though many black people faced impediments to voting until the 1960s through intimidation and local voting restrictions.

Supreme Court: the United States federal court that acts as the chief interpreter of the nation's constitution; the court holds ultimate power over all federal and state courts. It considers any attempt by states to nullify its laws as unconstitutional.

Thirteenth Amendment: the constitutional Amendment that formally abolished slavery and forced labor, except as punishment for a crime.

Union: the United States was often referred to as "the Union" during the American Civil War. Then-president Abraham Lincoln defended this against the secession of some Southern states.

Vagrancy: the act of moving from one place to another; not having a permanent home.

White supremacy: the belief that whites are superior to black people or others and therefore should have the right to dominate them.

World War II (1939–45): a global conflict fought between the Axis powers (Germany, Italy, and Japan) and the victorious Allied powers (the United Kingdom and its colonies, France, the Soviet Union, and the United States).

PEOPLE MENTIONED IN THE TEXT

Martha Abreu is an associate professor in the department of history at the Universidade Federal Fluminense in Brazil. She is a scholar of popular culture and social history, and has authored several important works in Portuguese, including *Meninas Perdidas: Os Populares e o Cotidiano do Amor na Belle Époque Carioca* (1989).

Bruce Baker is lecturer of American history at Newcastle University in the UK. He has written several important works, including *What Reconstruction Meant: Historical Memory in the American South* (2007).

Howard Beale (1899–1959) was professor of history at the University of North Carolina. His book *The Critical Year: A Study of Andrew Johnson and Reconstruction* (1930) was a major contribution to the discipline of history.

Charles Beard (1874–1948) was professor of history at Columbia University. One of the most renowned American historians, he published hundreds of important works, including *History of the United States* (1921).

Franz Boas (1858–1942) was professor of anthropology at Columbia University. The author of *Race, Language and Culture* (1940), he was one of the major opponents of the idea that race was a biological concept and black people were inherently inferior to whites.

Claude Bowers (1878–1958) was an American historian and member of the Democratic Party. Bowers's *The Tragic Era* (1929) was grounded in the Dunning School and argued that Reconstruction was tragic for the South.

Stephen Budiansky (b. 1957) is an American historian and author. His book *The Bloody Shirt: Terror after the Civil War* (2007) is an important contribution to our understanding of terrorist violence during the era of Reconstruction.

John Burgess (1844–1931) was an American political scientist and professor at Columbia University. He had a strong influence on the Dunning School.

Charles Darwin (1809–82) was an English naturalist and the author of *On the Origin of Species* (1859) and *The Descent of Man* (1871). Darwin argued that the "white and black races" differed from each other in intellectual capability, a view that has since been discredited.

David Brion Davis (b. 1927) is one of the most important contemporary historians on the eras of slavery and abolition. He has written numerous important works, including *The Problem of Slavery in Western Culture* (1966) and *The Problem of Slavery in the Age of Revolution* (1975).

Frederick Douglass (1818–95) was an escaped slave who became a prominent abolitionist, author, and public speaker. He wrote several important works, including *My Bondage and My Freedom* (1855), that served as a source of inspiration for future civil rights activists, such as W. E. B. Du Bois.

W. E. B. Du Bois (1868–1963) was a sociologist, historian, author, and civil rights activist. His book *The Souls of Black Folk* (1903) was one of the first sociological explorations of the African American experience.

William A. Dunning (1857–1922) was an American historian and professor at Columbia University. He and others developed the

Dunning School (of Reconstruction) which argued that granting black people the right to vote and hold office was a serious error because they were unprepared for and incapable of handling such responsibility. This perspective helped sustain Jim Crow.

Demetrius Eudell is professor of history at Wesleyan University. He is a scholar of slavery, abolition, and emancipation, and the author of *Political Languages of Emancipation in the British Caribbean and the U.S. South* (2002).

Jack Foner (1910–99) was an American historian and a professor at City University of New York. He was a scholar of African American history and labor movements, and the author of *Black People and the Military in American History* (1974).

Philip Foner (1910–94) was an American Marxist labor historian and teacher, best known for his 10-volume *History of the Labor Movement in the United States* (1947–94) and for *The Life and Writings of Frederick Douglass* (1975).

Thavolia Glymph (b. 1951) is associate professor of African and African American studies at Duke University. She is the author of several important works, including *Out of the House of Bondage: The Transformation of the Plantation Household* (2008).

Ulysses S. Grant (1822–85) was the 18th president of the United States between 1869 and 1877. A Republican, his term coincided with the Reconstruction period.

Freddie Gray (1989–2015) was a black resident of Baltimore, Maryland, who died from a spinal cord injury while in police custody in April 2015.

D. W. Griffith (1875–1948) was an American film director. In 1915, he directed *The Birth of a Nation*, in which he portrayed black men as stupid and sexually aggressive toward white women, and the Ku Klux Klan as the saving grace for whites.

Steven Hahn (b. 1951) is Roy F. and Jeannette P. Nichols professor in American history at the University of Pennsylvania. He has written several important works, including *The Roots of Southern Populism: Yeoman Farmers and the Transformation of the Georgia Upcountry, 1850–1890* (1983).

Rutherford B. Hayes (1822–93) was the 19th president of the United States. In 1877, he withdrew Northern troops from the South, bringing an end to Reconstruction.

Richard Hofstadter (1916–70) was an American historian and public intellectual. Eric Foner's PhD supervisor, he was the Dewitt Clinton Professor of American History at Columbia University prior to Foner, and wrote several important works, including *Social Darwinism in American Thought* (1944).

Thomas Jefferson (1743–1826) was the main author of the Declaration of Independence and became the third president of the United States. Jefferson advocated a government with numerous branches—executive, legislative, and judicial—believing that a separation of powers between these branches would help prevent government abuse and oppression.

Andrew Johnson (1808–75) was the 17th president of the United States. Replacing Abraham Lincoln after his assassination, Johnson led Reconstruction from 1865 to 1869.

Nicholas Lemann (b. 1954) is an American historian and journalist. He is Joseph Pulitzer II and Edith Pulitzer Moore Professor of Journalism and dean emeritus at Columbia University Journalism School, and the author of *Redemption: The Last Battle of the Civil War* (2006).

Abraham Lincoln (1809–65) was the 16th president of the United States. He issued the Emancipation Proclamation in 1863, formally ending slavery in the US.

Hebe Mattos is professor of history and coordinator of the LABHOI/UFF Memory of Slavery Oral History Project at the University Federal Fluminense in Brazil.

Richard Morris (1904–89) was an American historian and scholar of American law and the American Revolution. He wrote several important works, including *The American Revolution Reconsidered* (1966).

Barack Obama (b. 1961) is the 44th president of the United States and the first African American to hold this office.

Thomas Paine (1737–1809) was an English pamphleteer and supporter of the American and French Revolutions. He was a proponent of natural rights and universal equality, and rejected slavery.

Michael Perman (b. 1942) is emeritus professor of history at the University of Illinois at Chicago. He is a scholar of the American Civil War and Reconstruction, and the author of several important works, including *Struggle for Mastery: Disfranchisement in the South, 1888–1908* (2001).

Ulrich Phillips (1877–1934) was a professor at Columbia University and student of William A. Dunning. The author of *American Negro Slavery* (1918) and *Life and Labor in the Old South* (1929), he was an influential historian who argued that, although slavery was a harsh system, it was necessary to civilize blacks.

Heather Cox Richardson is professor of history at Boston College. She is a scholar of nineteenth-century American history, and the author of *West from Appomattox: The Reconstruction of America after the Civil War* (2007).

Bernie Sanders (b. 1941) is US senator for the state of Vermont. A Democrat, he is a presidential candidate in 2016.

James Shenton (1925–2003) was professor of history at Columbia University from 1951 to 1996. He is the author of several important works, including *The Historian's History of the United States* (1966).

Herbert Spencer (1820–1903) was an English philosopher and sociologist. The author of *The Synthetic Philosophy* (1896), he adapted Charles Darwin's ideas regarding evolutionary biology to the social sciences, claiming that whites were innately superior to blacks.

Kenneth Stampp (1912–2009) was Alexander F. and May T. Morrison Professor of History Emeritus at the University of California, Berkeley. He was a scholar of slavery, the American Civil War, and Reconstruction, and the author of several important works, including *The Era of Reconstruction, 1865–1877* (1965).

C. Vann Woodward (1908–99) was professor of history at Yale University and a scholar of the American South and race relations. He wrote several important works, including *Origins of the New South, 1877–1913* (1951) and *The Strange Career of Jim Crow* (1955).

WORKS CITED

WORKS CITED

Baker, Bruce. *What Reconstruction Meant*. Charlottesville, VA: University of Virginia Press, 2007.

Budiansky, Stephen. *The Bloody Shirt: Terror after Appomattox*. New York: Viking, 2008.

Du Bois, W. E. B. *Black Reconstruction in America*. London: Transaction Publishers, 2013.

Eudell, Demetrius L. *Political Languages of Emancipation in the British Caribbean and the U.S. South*. Chapel Hill: University of North Carolina Press, 2002.

Foner, Eric. *The Fiery Trial: Abraham Lincoln and American Slavery*. New York: W. W. Norton, 2010.

_____.*Free Soil, Free Labor, Free Men*. New York: Oxford University Press, 1995.

— — —."The New View of Reconstruction." *American Heritage* 34, no. 6 (1983).

_____.*Nothing but Freedom: Emancipation and Its Legacy*. Baton Rouge: Louisiana State University Press. 1983.

_____.*Our Lincoln: New Perspectives on Lincoln and His World*. New York: W. W. Norton, 2008.

_____.*Reconstruction: America's Unfinished Revolution, 1863–1877*. New York: HarperCollins, 2014.

_____.*The Story of American Freedom*. New York: W. W. Norton, 1998.

_____.*Who Owns History? Rethinking the Past in a Changing World*. New York: Hill and Wang, 2002.

Gao, George. "Chart of the Week: The Black–White Gap in Incarceration Rates." *Pew Research Center*, July 18, 2014. Accessed January 10, 2015. http://www.pewresearch.org/fact-tank/2014/07/18/chart-of-the-week-the-black-white-gap-in-incarceration-rates/

Glymph, Thavolia. *Out of the House of Bondage: The Transformation of the Plantation Household*. Cambridge: Cambridge University Press, 2008.

Goodman, Amy, and Juan González. "Civil War Historian Eric Foner on the Radical Possibilities of Reconstruction." *Democracy Now*, March 11, 2015. Accessed December 9, 2015. http://www.democracynow.org/blog/2015/3/11/civil_war_historian_eric_foner_on

Hahn, Steven. *A Nation under Our Feet*. Cambridge, MA: Belknap Press, 2003.

———."The Other American Revolution: A Book Review of *Forever Free: The Story of Emancipation and Reconstruction* by Eric Foner." *New Republic Online*. Accessed January 10, 2016. http://inside.sfuhs.org/dept/history/US_History_reader/Chapter6/reviewoffoner.htm

Irwin, Neil, Claire Cain Miller, and Margot Sanger-Katz. "America's Racial Divide, Chartered." *New York Times*, August 19, 2014. Accessed January 10, 2015, http://www.nytimes.com/2014/08/20/upshot/americas-racial-divide-charted.html?_r=0

Konczal, Mike. "How Radical Change Occurs: An Interview with Historian Eric Foner." *The Nation*, February 3, 2015. Accessed December 9, 2015. http://www.thenation.com/article/how-radical-change-occurs-interview-historian-eric-foner/

Lemann, Nicholas. *Redemption: The Last Battle of the Civil War*. New York: Farrar, Straus and Giroux, 2006.

Lincoln, Abraham. "Gettysburg Address," November 19, 1863. Accessed January 10, 2016. http://www.abrahamlincolnonline.org/lincoln/speeches/gettysburg.htm

Perman, Michael. "Eric Foner's Reconstruction: A Finished Revolution." *Reviews in American History* 17, no. 1 (1989): 73–8.

Richardson, Heather Cox. *West from Appomattox: The Reconstruction of America after the Civil War*. New Haven, CT: Yale University Press, 2007.

Stampp, Kenneth M. *The Era of Reconstruction, 1865–1877*. New York: Knopf, 1965.

———.*The Peculiar Institution: Slavery in the Ante-Bellum South*. New York: Knopf, 1956.

Watkin, Eric. "Professor James P. Shenton '49: History's Happy Warrior." *Columbia College Today* 22, no. 3 (1996).

THE MACAT LIBRARY
BY DISCIPLINE

AFRICANA STUDIES

Chinua Achebe's *An Image of Africa: Racism in Conrad's Heart of Darkness*
W. E. B. Du Bois's *The Souls of Black Folk*
Zora Neale Huston's *Characteristics of Negro Expression*
Martin Luther King Jr's *Why We Can't Wait*
Toni Morrison's *Playing in the Dark: Whiteness in the American Literary Imagination*

ANTHROPOLOGY

Arjun Appadurai's *Modernity at Large: Cultural Dimensions of Globalisation*
Philippe Ariès's *Centuries of Childhood*
Franz Boas's *Race, Language and Culture*
Kim Chan & Renée Mauborgne's *Blue Ocean Strategy*
Jared Diamond's *Guns, Germs & Steel: the Fate of Human Societies*
Jared Diamond's *Collapse: How Societies Choose to Fail or Survive*
E. E. Evans-Pritchard's *Witchcraft, Oracles and Magic Among the Azande*
James Ferguson's *The Anti-Politics Machine*
Clifford Geertz's *The Interpretation of Cultures*
David Graeber's *Debt: the First 5000 Years*
Karen Ho's *Liquidated: An Ethnography of Wall Street*
Geert Hofstede's *Culture's Consequences: Comparing Values, Behaviors, Institutes and Organizations across Nations*
Claude Lévi-Strauss's *Structural Anthropology*
Jay Macleod's *Ain't No Makin' It: Aspirations and Attainment in a Low-Income Neighborhood*
Saba Mahmood's *The Politics of Piety: The Islamic Revival and the Feminist Subject*
Marcel Mauss's *The Gift*

BUSINESS

Jean Lave & Etienne Wenger's *Situated Learning*
Theodore Levitt's *Marketing Myopia*
Burton G. Malkiel's *A Random Walk Down Wall Street*
Douglas McGregor's *The Human Side of Enterprise*
Michael Porter's *Competitive Strategy: Creating and Sustaining Superior Performance*
John Kotter's *Leading Change*
C. K. Prahalad & Gary Hamel's *The Core Competence of the Corporation*

CRIMINOLOGY

Michelle Alexander's *The New Jim Crow: Mass Incarceration in the Age of Colorblindness*
Michael R. Gottfredson & Travis Hirschi's *A General Theory of Crime*
Richard Herrnstein & Charles A. Murray's *The Bell Curve: Intelligence and Class Structure in American Life*
Elizabeth Loftus's *Eyewitness Testimony*
Jay Macleod's *Ain't No Makin' It: Aspirations and Attainment in a Low-Income Neighborhood*
Philip Zimbardo's *The Lucifer Effect*

ECONOMICS

Janet Abu-Lughod's *Before European Hegemony*
Ha-Joon Chang's *Kicking Away the Ladder*
David Brion Davis's *The Problem of Slavery in the Age of Revolution*
Milton Friedman's *The Role of Monetary Policy*
Milton Friedman's *Capitalism and Freedom*
David Graeber's *Debt: the First 5000 Years*
Friedrich Hayek's *The Road to Serfdom*
Karen Ho's *Liquidated: An Ethnography of Wall Street*

John Maynard Keynes's *The General Theory of Employment, Interest and Money*
Charles P. Kindleberger's *Manias, Panics and Crashes*
Robert Lucas's *Why Doesn't Capital Flow from Rich to Poor Countries?*
Burton G. Malkiel's *A Random Walk Down Wall Street*
Thomas Robert Malthus's *An Essay on the Principle of Population*
Karl Marx's *Capital*
Thomas Piketty's *Capital in the Twenty-First Century*
Amartya Sen's *Development as Freedom*
Adam Smith's *The Wealth of Nations*
Nassim Nicholas Taleb's *The Black Swan: The Impact of the Highly Improbable*
Amos Tversky's & Daniel Kahneman's *Judgment under Uncertainty: Heuristics and Biases*
Mahbub Ul Haq's *Reflections on Human Development*
Max Weber's *The Protestant Ethic and the Spirit of Capitalism*

FEMINISM AND GENDER STUDIES

Judith Butler's *Gender Trouble*
Simone De Beauvoir's *The Second Sex*
Michel Foucault's *History of Sexuality*
Betty Friedan's *The Feminine Mystique*
Saba Mahmood's *The Politics of Piety: The Islamic Revival and the Feminist Subjec*t
Joan Wallach Scott's *Gender and the Politics of History*
Mary Wollstonecraft's *A Vindication of the Rights of Woman*
Virginia Woolf's *A Room of One's Own*

GEOGRAPHY

The Brundtland Report's *Our Common Future*
Rachel Carson's *Silent Spring*
Charles Darwin's *On the Origin of Species*
James Ferguson's *The Anti-Politics Machine*
Jane Jacobs's *The Death and Life of Great American Cities*
James Lovelock's *Gaia: A New Look at Life on Earth*
Amartya Sen's *Development as Freedom*
Mathis Wackernagel & William Rees's *Our Ecological Footprint*

HISTORY

Janet Abu-Lughod's *Before European Hegemony*
Benedict Anderson's *Imagined Communities*
Bernard Bailyn's *The Ideological Origins of the American Revolution*
Hanna Batatu's *The Old Social Classes And The Revolutionary Movements Of Iraq*
Christopher Browning's *Ordinary Men: Reserve Police Batallion 101 and the Final Solution in Poland*
Edmund Burke's *Reflections on the Revolution in France*
William Cronon's *Nature's Metropolis: Chicago And The Great West*
Alfred W. Crosby's *The Columbian Exchange*
Hamid Dabashi's *Iran: A People Interrupted*
David Brion Davis's *The Problem of Slavery in the Age of Revolution*
Nathalie Zemon Davis's *The Return of Martin Guerre*
Jared Diamond's *Guns, Germs & Steel: the Fate of Human Societies*
Frank Dikotter's *Mao's Great Famine*
John W Dower's *War Without Mercy: Race And Power In The Pacific War*
W. E. B. Du Bois's *The Souls of Black Folk*
Richard J. Evans's *In Defence of History*
Lucien Febvre's *The Problem of Unbelief in the 16th Century*
Sheila Fitzpatrick's *Everyday Stalinism*

The Macat Library By Discipline

Eric Foner's *Reconstruction: America's Unfinished Revolution, 1863-1877*
Michel Foucault's *Discipline and Punish*
Michel Foucault's *History of Sexuality*
Francis Fukuyama's *The End of History and the Last Man*
John Lewis Gaddis's *We Now Know: Rethinking Cold War History*
Ernest Gellner's *Nations and Nationalism*
Eugene Genovese's *Roll, Jordan, Roll: The World the Slaves Made*
Carlo Ginzburg's *The Night Battles*
Daniel Goldhagen's *Hitler's Willing Executioners*
Jack Goldstone's *Revolution and Rebellion in the Early Modern World*
Antonio Gramsci's *The Prison Notebooks*
Alexander Hamilton, John Jay & James Madison's *The Federalist Papers*
Christopher Hill's *The World Turned Upside Down*
Carole Hillenbrand's *The Crusades: Islamic Perspectives*
Thomas Hobbes's *Leviathan*
Eric Hobsbawm's *The Age Of Revolution*
John A. Hobson's *Imperialism: A Study*
Albert Hourani's *History of the Arab Peoples*
Samuel P. Huntington's *The Clash of Civilizations and the Remaking of World Order*
C. L. R. James's *The Black Jacobins*
Tony Judt's *Postwar: A History of Europe Since 1945*
Ernst Kantorowicz's *The King's Two Bodies: A Study in Medieval Political Theology*
Paul Kennedy's *The Rise and Fall of the Great Powers*
Ian Kershaw's *The "Hitler Myth": Image and Reality in the Third Reich*
John Maynard Keynes's *The General Theory of Employment, Interest and Money*
Charles P. Kindleberger's *Manias, Panics and Crashes*
Martin Luther King Jr's *Why We Can't Wait*
Henry Kissinger's *World Order: Reflections on the Character of Nations and the Course of History*
Thomas Kuhn's *The Structure of Scientific Revolutions*
Georges Lefebvre's *The Coming of the French Revolution*
John Locke's *Two Treatises of Government*
Niccolò Machiavelli's *The Prince*
Thomas Robert Malthus's *An Essay on the Principle of Population*
Mahmood Mamdani's *Citizen and Subject: Contemporary Africa And The Legacy Of Late Colonialism*
Karl Marx's *Capital*
Stanley Milgram's *Obedience to Authority*
John Stuart Mill's *On Liberty*
Thomas Paine's *Common Sense*
Thomas Paine's *Rights of Man*
Geoffrey Parker's *Global Crisis: War, Climate Change and Catastrophe in the Seventeenth Century*
Jonathan Riley-Smith's *The First Crusade and the Idea of Crusading*
Jean-Jacques Rousseau's *The Social Contract*
Joan Wallach Scott's *Gender and the Politics of History*
Theda Skocpol's *States and Social Revolutions*
Adam Smith's *The Wealth of Nations*
Timothy Snyder's *Bloodlands: Europe Between Hitler and Stalin*
Sun Tzu's *The Art of War*
Keith Thomas's *Religion and the Decline of Magic*
Thucydides's *The History of the Peloponnesian War*
Frederick Jackson Turner's *The Significance of the Frontier in American History*
Odd Arne Westad's *The Global Cold War: Third World Interventions And The Making Of Our Times*

LITERATURE

Chinua Achebe's *An Image of Africa: Racism in Conrad's Heart of Darkness*
Roland Barthes's *Mythologies*
Homi K. Bhabha's *The Location of Culture*
Judith Butler's *Gender Trouble*
Simone De Beauvoir's *The Second Sex*
Ferdinand De Saussure's *Course in General Linguistics*
T. S. Eliot's *The Sacred Wood: Essays on Poetry and Criticism*
Zora Neale Huston's *Characteristics of Negro Expression*
Toni Morrison's *Playing in the Dark: Whiteness in the American Literary Imagination*
Edward Said's *Orientalism*
Gayatri Chakravorty Spivak's *Can the Subaltern Speak?*
Mary Wollstonecraft's *A Vindication of the Rights of Women*
Virginia Woolf's *A Room of One's Own*

PHILOSOPHY

Elizabeth Anscombe's *Modern Moral Philosophy*
Hannah Arendt's *The Human Condition*
Aristotle's *Metaphysics*
Aristotle's *Nicomachean Ethics*
Edmund Gettier's *Is Justified True Belief Knowledge?*
Georg Wilhelm Friedrich Hegel's *Phenomenology of Spirit*
David Hume's *Dialogues Concerning Natural Religion*
David Hume's *The Enquiry for Human Understanding*
Immanuel Kant's *Religion within the Boundaries of Mere Reason*
Immanuel Kant's *Critique of Pure Reason*
Søren Kierkegaard's *The Sickness Unto Death*
Søren Kierkegaard's *Fear and Trembling*
C. S. Lewis's *The Abolition of Man*
Alasdair MacIntyre's *After Virtue*
Marcus Aurelius's *Meditations*
Friedrich Nietzsche's *On the Genealogy of Morality*
Friedrich Nietzsche's *Beyond Good and Evil*
Plato's *Republic*
Plato's *Symposium*
Jean-Jacques Rousseau's *The Social Contract*
Gilbert Ryle's *The Concept of Mind*
Baruch Spinoza's *Ethics*
Sun Tzu's *The Art of War*
Ludwig Wittgenstein's *Philosophical Investigations*

POLITICS

Benedict Anderson's *Imagined Communities*
Aristotle's *Politics*
Bernard Bailyn's *The Ideological Origins of the American Revolution*
Edmund Burke's *Reflections on the Revolution in France*
John C. Calhoun's *A Disquisition on Government*
Ha-Joon Chang's *Kicking Away the Ladder*
Hamid Dabashi's *Iran: A People Interrupted*
Hamid Dabashi's *Theology of Discontent: The Ideological Foundation of the Islamic Revolution in Iran*
Robert Dahl's *Democracy and its Critics*
Robert Dahl's *Who Governs?*
David Brion Davis's *The Problem of Slavery in the Age of Revolution*

Alexis De Tocqueville's *Democracy in America*
James Ferguson's *The Anti-Politics Machine*
Frank Dikotter's *Mao's Great Famine*
Sheila Fitzpatrick's *Everyday Stalinism*
Eric Foner's *Reconstruction: America's Unfinished Revolution, 1863-1877*
Milton Friedman's *Capitalism and Freedom*
Francis Fukuyama's *The End of History and the Last Man*
John Lewis Gaddis's *We Now Know: Rethinking Cold War History*
Ernest Gellner's *Nations and Nationalism*
David Graeber's *Debt: the First 5000 Years*
Antonio Gramsci's *The Prison Notebooks*
Alexander Hamilton, John Jay & James Madison's *The Federalist Papers*
Friedrich Hayek's *The Road to Serfdom*
Christopher Hill's *The World Turned Upside Down*
Thomas Hobbes's *Leviathan*
John A. Hobson's *Imperialism: A Study*
Samuel P. Huntington's *The Clash of Civilizations and the Remaking of World Order*
Tony Judt's *Postwar: A History of Europe Since 1945*
David C. Kang's *China Rising: Peace, Power and Order in East Asia*
Paul Kennedy's *The Rise and Fall of Great Powers*
Robert Keohane's *After Hegemony*
Martin Luther King Jr.'s *Why We Can't Wait*
Henry Kissinger's *World Order: Reflections on the Character of Nations and the Course of History*
John Locke's *Two Treatises of Government*
Niccolò Machiavelli's *The Prince*
Thomas Robert Malthus's *An Essay on the Principle of Population*
Mahmood Mamdani's *Citizen and Subject: Contemporary Africa And The Legacy Of Late Colonialism*
Karl Marx's *Capital*
John Stuart Mill's *On Liberty*
John Stuart Mill's *Utilitarianism*
Hans Morgenthau's *Politics Among Nations*
Thomas Paine's *Common Sense*
Thomas Paine's *Rights of Man*
Thomas Piketty's *Capital in the Twenty-First Century*
Robert D. Putman's *Bowling Alone*
John Rawls's *Theory of Justice*
Jean-Jacques Rousseau's *The Social Contract*
Theda Skocpol's *States and Social Revolutions*
Adam Smith's *The Wealth of Nations*
Sun Tzu's *The Art of War*
Henry David Thoreau's *Civil Disobedience*
Thucydides's *The History of the Peloponnesian War*
Kenneth Waltz's *Theory of International Politics*
Max Weber's *Politics as a Vocation*
Odd Arne Westad's *The Global Cold War: Third World Interventions And The Making Of Our Times*

POSTCOLONIAL STUDIES

Roland Barthes's *Mythologies*
Frantz Fanon's *Black Skin, White Masks*
Homi K. Bhabha's *The Location of Culture*
Gustavo Gutiérrez's *A Theology of Liberation*
Edward Said's *Orientalism*
Gayatri Chakravorty Spivak's *Can the Subaltern Speak?*

PSYCHOLOGY

Gordon Allport's *The Nature of Prejudice*
Alan Baddeley & Graham Hitch's *Aggression: A Social Learning Analysis*
Albert Bandura's *Aggression: A Social Learning Analysis*
Leon Festinger's *A Theory of Cognitive Dissonance*
Sigmund Freud's *The Interpretation of Dreams*
Betty Friedan's *The Feminine Mystique*
Michael R. Gottfredson & Travis Hirschi's *A General Theory of Crime*
Eric Hoffer's *The True Believer: Thoughts on the Nature of Mass Movements*
William James's *Principles of Psychology*
Elizabeth Loftus's *Eyewitness Testimony*
A. H. Maslow's *A Theory of Human Motivation*
Stanley Milgram's *Obedience to Authority*
Steven Pinker's *The Better Angels of Our Nature*
Oliver Sacks's *The Man Who Mistook His Wife For a Hat*
Richard Thaler & Cass Sunstein's *Nudge: Improving Decisions About Health, Wealth and Happiness*
Amos Tversky's *Judgment under Uncertainty: Heuristics and Biases*
Philip Zimbardo's *The Lucifer Effect*

SCIENCE

Rachel Carson's *Silent Spring*
William Cronon's *Nature's Metropolis: Chicago And The Great West*
Alfred W. Crosby's *The Columbian Exchange*
Charles Darwin's *On the Origin of Species*
Richard Dawkin's *The Selfish Gene*
Thomas Kuhn's *The Structure of Scientific Revolutions*
Geoffrey Parker's *Global Crisis: War, Climate Change and Catastrophe in the Seventeenth Century*
Mathis Wackernagel & William Rees's *Our Ecological Footprint*

SOCIOLOGY

Michelle Alexander's *The New Jim Crow: Mass Incarceration in the Age of Colorblindness*
Gordon Allport's *The Nature of Prejudice*
Albert Bandura's *Aggression: A Social Learning Analysis*
Hanna Batatu's *The Old Social Classes And The Revolutionary Movements Of Iraq*
Ha-Joon Chang's *Kicking Away the Ladder*
W. E. B. Du Bois's *The Souls of Black Folk*
Émile Durkheim's *On Suicide*
Frantz Fanon's *Black Skin, White Masks*
Frantz Fanon's *The Wretched of the Earth*
Eric Foner's *Reconstruction: America's Unfinished Revolution, 1863-1877*
Eugene Genovese's *Roll, Jordan, Roll: The World the Slaves Made*
Jack Goldstone's *Revolution and Rebellion in the Early Modern World*
Antonio Gramsci's *The Prison Notebooks*
Richard Herrnstein & Charles A Murray's *The Bell Curve: Intelligence and Class Structure in American Life*
Eric Hoffer's *The True Believer: Thoughts on the Nature of Mass Movements*
Jane Jacobs's *The Death and Life of Great American Cities*
Robert Lucas's *Why Doesn't Capital Flow from Rich to Poor Countries?*
Jay Macleod's *Ain't No Makin' It: Aspirations and Attainment in a Low Income Neighborhood*
Elaine May's *Homeward Bound: American Families in the Cold War Era*
Douglas McGregor's *The Human Side of Enterprise*
C. Wright Mills's *The Sociological Imagination*

The Macat Library By Discipline

Thomas Piketty's *Capital in the Twenty-First Century*
Robert D. Putman's *Bowling Alone*
David Riesman's *The Lonely Crowd: A Study of the Changing American Character*
Edward Said's *Orientalism*
Joan Wallach Scott's *Gender and the Politics of History*
Theda Skocpol's *States and Social Revolutions*
Max Weber's *The Protestant Ethic and the Spirit of Capitalism*

THEOLOGY

Augustine's *Confessions*
Benedict's *Rule of St Benedict*
Gustavo Gutiérrez's *A Theology of Liberation*
Carole Hillenbrand's *The Crusades: Islamic Perspectives*
David Hume's *Dialogues Concerning Natural Religion*
Immanuel Kant's *Religion within the Boundaries of Mere Reason*
Ernst Kantorowicz's *The King's Two Bodies: A Study in Medieval Political Theology*
Søren Kierkegaard's *The Sickness Unto Death*
C. S. Lewis's *The Abolition of Man*
Saba Mahmood's *The Politics of Piety: The Islamic Revival and the Feminist Subject*
Baruch Spinoza's *Ethics*
Keith Thomas's *Religion and the Decline of Magic*

COMING SOON

Chris Argyris's *The Individual and the Organisation*
Seyla Benhabib's *The Rights of Others*
Walter Benjamin's *The Work Of Art in the Age of Mechanical Reproduction*
John Berger's *Ways of Seeing*
Pierre Bourdieu's *Outline of a Theory of Practice*
Mary Douglas's *Purity and Danger*
Roland Dworkin's *Taking Rights Seriously*
James G. March's *Exploration and Exploitation in Organisational Learning*
Ikujiro Nonaka's *A Dynamic Theory of Organizational Knowledge Creation*
Griselda Pollock's *Vision and Difference*
Amartya Sen's *Inequality Re-Examined*
Susan Sontag's *On Photography*
Yasser Tabbaa's *The Transformation of Islamic Art*
Ludwig von Mises's *Theory of Money and Credit*

Macat Disciplines

Access the greatest ideas and thinkers across entire disciplines, including

AFRICANA STUDIES

Chinua Achebe's *An Image of Africa: Racism in Conrad's Heart of Darkness*

W. E. B. Du Bois's *The Souls of Black Folk*

Zora Neale Hurston's *Characteristics of Negro Expression*

Martin Luther King Jr.'s *Why We Can't Wait*

Toni Morrison's *Playing in the Dark: Whiteness in the American Literary Imagination*

Macat analyses are available from all good bookshops and libraries.

Access hundreds of analyses through one, multimedia tool. Join free for one month **library.macat.com**

Macat Disciplines

Access the greatest ideas and thinkers across entire disciplines, including

FEMINISM, GENDER AND QUEER STUDIES

Simone De Beauvoir's
The Second Sex

Michel Foucault's
History of Sexuality

Betty Friedan's
The Feminine Mystique

Saba Mahmood's
*The Politics of Piety:
The Islamic Revival and
the Feminist Subject*

Joan Wallach Scott's
*Gender and the
Politics of History*

Mary Wollstonecraft's
*A Vindication of the
Rights of Woman*

Virginia Woolf's
A Room of One's Own

Judith Butler's
Gender Trouble

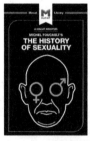

Macat analyses are available from all good bookshops and libraries.

Access hundreds of analyses through one, multimedia tool.
Join free for one month **library.macat.com**

Macat Disciplines

Access the greatest ideas and thinkers across entire disciplines, including

INEQUALITY

Ha-Joon Chang's, *Kicking Away the Ladder*
David Graeber's, *Debt: The First 5000 Years*
Robert E. Lucas's, *Why Doesn't Capital Flow from Rich To Poor Countries?*
Thomas Piketty's, *Capital in the Twenty-First Century*
Amartya Sen's, *Inequality Re-Examined*
Mahbub Ul Haq's, *Reflections on Human Development*

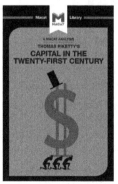

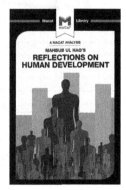

Macat analyses are available from all good bookshops and libraries.

Access hundreds of analyses through one, multimedia tool.
Join free for one month **library.macat.com**

Macat Disciplines

Access the greatest ideas and thinkers across entire disciplines, including

CRIMINOLOGY

Michelle Alexander's
The New Jim Crow:
Mass Incarceration in the
Age of Colorblindness

Michael R. Gottfredson
& Travis Hirschi's
A General Theory of Crime

Elizabeth Loftus's
Eyewitness Testimony

Richard Herrnstein
& Charles A. Murray's
The Bell Curve: Intelligence and
Class Structure in American Life

Jay Macleod's
Ain't No Makin' It:
Aspirations and Attainment in a
Low-Income Neighborhood

Philip Zimbardo's
The Lucifer Effect

Macat analyses are available from all good bookshops and libraries.

Access hundreds of analyses through one, multimedia tool.
Join free for one month **library.macat.com**

Macat Disciplines

Access the greatest ideas and thinkers across entire disciplines, including

Postcolonial Studies

Roland Barthes's *Mythologies*
Frantz Fanon's *Black Skin, White Masks*
Homi K. Bhabha's *The Location of Culture*
Gustavo Gutiérrez's *A Theology of Liberation*
Edward Said's *Orientalism*
Gayatri Chakravorty Spivak's *Can the Subaltern Speak?*

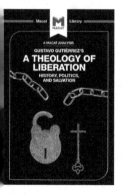

Macat analyses are available from all good bookshops and libraries.

Access hundreds of analyses through one, multimedia tool.
Join free for one month **library.macat.com**

Macat Disciplines

Access the greatest ideas and thinkers across entire disciplines, including

GLOBALIZATION

Arjun Appadurai's, *Modernity at Large: Cultural Dimensions of Globalisation*

James Ferguson's, *The Anti-Politics Machine*

Geert Hofstede's, *Culture's Consequences*

Amartya Sen's, *Development as Freedom*

Macat Pairs

Analyse historical and modern issues from opposite sides of an argument. Pairs include:

HOW TO RUN AN ECONOMY

John Maynard Keynes's
The General Theory OF Employment, Interest and Money

Classical economics suggests that market economies are self-correcting in times of recession or depression, and tend toward full employment and output. But English economist John Maynard Keynes disagrees.

In his ground-breaking 1936 study *The General Theory*, Keynes argues that traditional economics has misunderstood the causes of unemployment. Employment is not determined by the price of labor; it is directly linked to demand. Keynes believes market economies are by nature unstable, and so require government intervention. Spurred on by the social catastrophe of the Great Depression of the 1930s, he sets out to revolutionize the way the world thinks

Milton Friedman's
The Role of Monetary Policy

Friedman's 1968 paper changed the course of economic theory. In just 17 pages, he demolished existing theory and outlined an effective alternate monetary policy designed to secure 'high employment, stable prices and rapid growth.'

Friedman demonstrated that monetary policy plays a vital role in broader economic stability and argued that economists got their monetary policy wrong in the 1950s and 1960s by misunderstanding the relationship between inflation and unemployment. Previous generations of economists had believed that governments could permanently decrease unemployment by permitting inflation—and vice versa. Friedman's most original contribution was to show that this supposed trade-off is an illusion that only works in the short term.

Macat Disciplines

Access the greatest ideas and thinkers across entire disciplines, including

THE FUTURE OF DEMOCRACY

Robert A. Dahl's, *Democracy and Its Critics*
Robert A. Dahl's, *Who Governs?*
Alexis De Toqueville's, *Democracy in America*
Niccolò Machiavelli's, *The Prince*
John Stuart Mill's, *On Liberty*
Robert D. Putnam's, *Bowling Alone*
Jean-Jacques Rousseau's, *The Social Contract*
Henry David Thoreau's, *Civil Disobedience*

Macat Disciplines

Access the greatest ideas and thinkers across entire disciplines, including

TOTALITARIANISM

Sheila Fitzpatrick's, *Everyday Stalinism*
Ian Kershaw's, *The "Hitler Myth"*
Timothy Snyder's, *Bloodlands*

Macat Pairs

Analyse historical and modern issues from opposite sides of an argument. Pairs include:

RACE AND IDENTITY

Zora Neale Hurston's
Characteristics of Negro Expression

Using material collected on anthropological expeditions to the South, Zora Neale Hurston explains how expression in African American culture in the early twentieth century departs from the art of white America. At the time, African American art was often criticized for copying white culture. For Hurston, this criticism misunderstood how art works. European tradition views art as something fixed. But Hurston describes a creative process that is alive, ever-changing, and largely improvisational. She maintains that African American art works through a process called 'mimicry'—where an imitated object or verbal pattern, for example, is reshaped and altered until it becomes something new, novel—and worthy of attention.

Frantz Fanon's
Black Skin, White Masks

Black Skin, White Masks offers a radical analysis of the psychological effects of colonization on the colonized.

Fanon witnessed the effects of colonization first hand both in his birthplace, Martinique, and again later in life when he worked as a psychiatrist in another French colony, Algeria. His text is uncompromising in form and argument. He dissects the dehumanizing effects of colonialism, arguing that it destroys the native sense of identity, forcing people to adapt to an alien set of values—including a core belief that they are inferior. This results in deep psychological trauma.

Fanon's work played a pivotal role in the civil rights movements of the 1960s.

Macat analyses are available from all good bookshops and libraries.

Access hundreds of analyses through one, multimedia tool. Join free for one month **library.macat.com**

Macat Pairs

Analyse historical and modern issues from opposite sides of an argument. Pairs include:

INTERNATIONAL RELATIONS IN THE 21ST CENTURY

Samuel P. Huntington's
The Clash of Civilisations

In his highly influential 1996 book, Huntington offers a vision of a post-Cold War world in which conflict takes place not between competing ideologies but between cultures. The worst clash, he argues, will be between the Islamic world and the West: the West's arrogance and belief that its culture is a "gift" to the world will come into conflict with Islam's obstinacy and concern that its culture is under attack from a morally decadent "other."

Clash inspired much debate between different political schools of thought. But its greatest impact came in helping define American foreign policy in the wake of the 2001 terrorist attacks in New York and Washington.

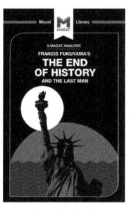

Francis Fukuyama's
The End of History and the Last Man

Published in 1992, *The End of History and the Last Man* argues that capitalist democracy is the final destination for all societies. Fukuyama believed democracy triumphed during the Cold War because it lacks the "fundamental contradictions" inherent in communism and satisfies our yearning for freedom and equality. Democracy therefore marks the endpoint in the evolution of ideology, and so the "end of history." There will still be "events," but no fundamental change in ideology.

Printed in the United States
by Baker & Taylor Publisher Services